iPhone 15
USER GUIDE

An Easy & Exhaustive Step-by-Step Manual for Non-Tech-Savvy. Discover the Best Tips & Tricks to Get the Max Out of Your New IPhone 15 in No Time!

Vin Mayer

© Copyright 2023
All rights reserved.
No part of this book may be reproduced or transmitted in any form or by any means, electronic or mechanical, including photocopying, recording, or by any information storage and retrieval system, without permission in writing from the publisher.

Disclaimer

The author and publisher have made every effort to ensure that the information in this book is accurate and up-to-date. However, the author and publisher disclaim all warranties, express or implied, with respect to the accuracy or completeness of the information contained in this book. The author and publisher shall not be liable for any damages arising out of or in connection with the use of this book.

Trademarks

iPhone, iPad, iOS, and macOS are registered trademarks of Apple Inc. All other trademarks mentioned in this book are the property of their respective owners.

TABLE OF CONTENTS

Introduction 11
Chapter 1: Setup and basics 12
    Turn on and set up iPhone 12
    Set Up Manually 13
    Wake and unlock 13
    Set up cellular service 13
    Apple ID and iCloud 14
Note: The applications chapter of this book contains an explanation of these processes. 15
Chapter 2: Personalize your iPhone 16
    Change sounds and vibrations 16
        turn vibration on or off on your iPhone 16
        How to create custom vibration pattern 16
    Create a custom Lock Screen 18
    How to Change your iphone wallpaper 20
        How to Quickly Set a Photo as Your Wallpaper 22
    screen brightness and color balance 23
        disable auto-brightness 23
    How to adjust the screen on time on iPhone 23
    How to magnify your screen 24
        Change the colour of the Zoom Controller 26
    Change the name of your iPhone 27
    Change the date and time 28
        How to Change Time on Your iPhone Automatically 28
        Change Time Zone on iPhone Automatically 29
        How to Change Time on Your iPhone Manually 30
    Change the language and region 31
        How to change language on iPhone 31
        How to Change Region On iPhone 31
    Set up Focus, notifications, and Do Not Disturb 32
        Setup Do Not Disturb 32
        How to Allow notifications 33
        Customize Focus Filters 35
        How to Enable Do Not Disturb from the Lock Screen 36
Chapter 3: Everything About The Latest Iphone 15 37
    iPhone 15-series price... 37
    Iphone 15 and USB-C 37

iPhone 15Dynamic Island and How to Use It 38
Can I Interact With Dynamic Island? 38
    Everything You Need to Know About 5x Optical Zoom of iPhone 15 Pro Max.. 39
    Customize the Action button on iPhone 15 Pro and iPhone 15 Pro Max 40
        Open a Camera Mode 40
        Use as a Shortcut or to Open Apps 41
        Activate an Accessibility Feature 41
    iPhone 15, Plus, Pro, Max new features 42
        How to Take Portrait Mode Photos on Iphone 15 42
        How to Turn Photos into Portraits After Shooting on Iphone 15 43
In photos, change the portrait effect 43
Simply open the picture again, choose Edit, and then select Revert to reverse any portrait effects........... 44
        How to Locate Friends With Precision Finding on Iphone 15 44
        How to stop Your iPhone 15 Battery from Charging Beyond 80% 45
        How to Charge Apple Watch, AirPods, or Another iPhone with your iphone 15 46
        How to Check Battery Cycle Count on iPhone 15 47
        How to Hard Reset the iPhone 15 (All Models) 47
        How to Hide the Silent Mode Bell Icon in the Status Bar 48
        How to Transfer Data Over USB-C at 10Gbps Speed on Iphone 15 48
        How to Adjust Camera Focal Length on iPhone 15 Pro.. 48
        How to Change Default Focal Length 49
        How to Disable Focal Length Presets 50
All you have to do is that. The 1x button will now always result in a 1x optical zoom. 50
Chapter 4: The Latest iOS 17 Version 51
To install iOS 17 on your iPhone, first make a backup. 51
    How to download and install iOS 17 52
    Lock Screen in iOS 17 53
        How to Use StandBy Mode.. 53
        How to Customize StandBy Mode in iOS 17 54
Add widgets to StandBy Mode 54
        How to Disable Standby Mode on iPhone 55
        How to Disable Notifications in StandBy Mode 55
        How to Change iPhone Clock Style in StandBy Mode 56
        How to Customize the Photos Screen in StandBy Mode 57
If you're satisfied, press Done. If not, tap the minus sign to the left of the album you just added. 57
        How to Disable the Red Tint in StandBy Mode 58
    Messages update ios 17 58
        How to Turn Live Photos into Animated Stickers in Messages 58
        How to Catch Up in a Messages Chat 59

How to Reorganize Your iMessage Apps 60
How to Delete iMessage Apps 60
The Delete button will show when you press the red minus sign next to a program. 61
How to Auto-Delete Verification Codes in Messages and Mail 61
How to Send an Audio Message in Apple's Messages App 61
How to Add Effects to Stickers in Messages 62
How to turn Emoji into Stickers in Messages 63
How to Share Your Location in the Messages App 64
How to Use ios 17 Check In Feature in Messages 64
Privacy and Security updates 66
How to Share Passwords With Friends and Family 66
How to Control Which Apps Have Access to Your Calendars 66
Safety 67
How to Manage Communication Safety for Your Child's iPhone 67
How to Enable Sensitive Content Warnings 68
Siri 68
How to Get Siri to Read Web Articles to You 68
How to Choose Which App Siri Uses to Send a Message 69
How to Force Siri to Listen for 'Hey Siri' Instead of Just 'Siri 70
Safari 70
How to Create a Safari Profile 70
How to Switch Between Profiles in Safari 71
How to Save Long-Form Web Articles and Other Scrollable Content to Photos on safari 71
How to Remove All URL Tracking in Safari on iPhone 72
How to Disable Private Browsing Authentication in Safari 73
How to Set a Different Default Search Engine When Private Browsing in Safari 73
How to Clear Safari Web History for a Specific Profile 73
Phone and FaceTime 74
How to Create Your Own Contact Poster 74
How to Record a FaceTime Video or Audio Message 75
How to Trigger Reaction Effects in FaceTime 76
New FaceTime Reactions 76
Gestures to Trigger Reactions 76
Autocorrect and the Keyboard 77
How to Use Predictive Autocorrect 77
Correcting Autocorrect 77
AirDrop 77
How to Send Files and Photos With AirDrop Proximity Sharing 77
Enable or Disable AirDrop Proximity Sharing 77

How to Share Contact Details With NameDrop. 78
   AirPlay.. 81
      How to Use Automatic AirPlay With Speakers.. 81
   Weather.. 82
Previous Day's Weather 82
Interface Tweaks 83
Module Changes 83
Moon Module 83
Daily Comparisons 84
Data Updates 84
      How to Switch Measurement Units in the Weather App 84
   Health... 84
      How to Track Your Mood With Health app.. 85

Get Reminders to Log Your State of Mind 86
      How to Get Follow Up and Critical Medication Reminders 86
      How to Protect Your Eyes With the Screen Distance Measuring Tool... 87
   Maps 88
      How to Download Offline Maps in Apple Maps 88
      Limited Service Warnings 88
For the time being, this function is only accessible for US National Parks. 88
      Electric Vehicle Charging Stations 89
      Interface Update 89
      Volume 89
Along with Add Stop, Share ETA, and Report an Incident, there is also a new volume option. 89
   Photos and Camera 89
      How to Name Your Pets in Photos With Pet Recognition 90
      How to Straighten Your Shooting Angle With the New Camera Level Feature... 90
      How to Enable the Camera Level 91
   Apple Music 91
      How to View Song Credits in Apple Music.. 92
      How to Crossfade Between Songs in Apple Music 92
   Notes and Reminders 93
      How to Create Links Between Apple Notes 93
      How to Sort Your Groceries in the Reminders App 93
   Other features 94
      How to Make Haptic Touch Faster on iPhone 94
      How to Change a New iPhone Passcode If You Forget It 95
      How to Set and Label Multiple Timers 96
      How to Find Your Apple TV Siri Remote Using Your iPhone 97

Find Your Siri Remote With Your iPhone ... 97
    How to set up Personal Voice on iOS 17 ... 98
    Using Personal Voice on iOS 17 ... 99
    How to share AirTags ... 100
    How to use audio message transcriptions ... 101

Chapter 5: Apps and Services ... 102
  Pre-installed Apps ... 102

App Store ... 102

Books ... 102

Calendar ... 102

Camera ... 102

Contacts ... 102

FaceTime ... 102

Files ... 102

Find My ... 102

Health ... 102

Mail ... 103

Maps ... 103

Notes ... 103

Phone ... 103

Photos ... 103

Safari ... 103

  How to use other apps and services ... 103
    Use App Clips ... 103

How do App Clips work? ... 104
    How to install new fonts on an iPhone ... 105
    How to use Freeform app ... 106

Freeform boards ... 106

Sticky notes ... 106

Freeform easy sharing ... 106
    How to use Find My ... 107
    How to Mark an Apple Device as Lost in the Find My App ... 107

Chapter 6: iPad, iWatch, and airpods ... 111
  ipadOS 17 ... 111
    iPadOS 17 features ... 111

With iPadOS 17, all of these essential functionalities are now accessible on the device. ... 111

Lock Screen ... 111

Interactive Widgets ... 111

Health ... 111

FaceTime	111
Messages	111
Stickers	112
PDFs and Notes	112
Safari	112
Keyboard	112
Freeform	112
Stage Manager	112
Spotlight	112
Photos	112
Siri	113
AirPlay	113
Find My	113
AirDrop	113
Reminders	113
Music	113
AirPods	113
Which iPads are compatible with iPadOS 17?	113
How To Install iPadOS 17	114
Apple Watch Series 9	114
new Double Tap gesture	114
Siri gets faster	115
Design	115
New watch bands	115
Battery	116
WatchOS 10	116
New design for widgets and applications	116
Snoopy is one of the new watch faces	117
How to get the Snoopy Watch Face using your iPhone	117
How to get the new Snoopy Watch Face on your Apple Watch without using an iPhone	119
Cycling, golf, and tennis modes	121
how to connect bike sensors – cadence, speed, power	121
Control Centre	121
Configuration & Calibration	122
How to Use Your iPhone to View Your Cycling Statistics	122
enhancements to Apple Maps	123
How to Use the Hiking Features in watchOS 10	123
Waypoints and Elevation Views	123
Looking for Nearby Trails	123

How to use topographical maps 124

The Apple Watch Series 9 can now more easily locate your iPhone. 128

Mental health and Mindfulness 128

Vision Health 128

AirPods Pro 128

How to Check Your AirPods Pro Firmware 128

Adaptive Audio 129

Under "Noise Control," tap Adaptive. 129

Conversation Awareness 130

Personalized Volume 130

Mute Controls 130

Chapter 7: CarPlay 132

Which iPhones are compatible with CarPlay? 132

Which cars offer CarPlay integration? 132

Can I get CarPlay in the car I already own? 132

How do you connect your iPhone to CarPlay? 133

How to set up wireless Apple CarPlay via USB 133

How to set up wireless Apple Carplay wirelessly 134

Do not worry if your vehicle does not support wired CarPlay or if you do not have a USB-A to Lightning cable on hand. Without a wire, you may install CarPlay by using the voice command capabilities of your vehicle. 134

While the wireless or Bluetooth is turned on, press and hold the voice command button on the steering wheel. 134

Go to Settings > General > CarPlay on your iPhone. 134

What apps work with CarPlay? 134

How is Siri integrated with CarPlay? 135

Chapter 8: Maintenance and Troubleshooting 136

Troubleshooting and Maintenance Practices 136

Restart Your iPhone 136

Update iOS 136

Go to Settings > General > Software upgrade to upgrade iOS. 136

Update Your Apps 136

Force-Close an iPhone App 136

The instance of an app can occasionally stop responding, causing it to freeze. 136

Force-Close an App on iPhone X or Later 136

Force-Close an App on iPhone SE, iPhone 8, or Earlier 136

Reset Your iPhone's Network Settings 137

Reset All Settings on Your iPhone 137

Factory Reset Your iPhone 137

Check Your iPhone's Battery Usage 138

Review Your iPhone's Battery Health 138

Fix Bluetooth Issues 138

Fix HomeKit Issues 138
Revoke Background Permissions 138
    Common Issues and Solutions 139
        iPhone Black Screen of Death 139
        Overheating Issues 139
        iPhone Camera Roll Crash 140
        iTunes Error 3194 140
        Wifi Is Not Getting Connected 140
        Cellular Connection Not Working on iPhone 140
        iPhone is Stuck at Apple Logo 141
        iPhone App Freezing/Crashing Randomly 141
        Damage Due To Water 141
Conclusion 143

INTRODUCTION

There are a few steps you must do to set up your iPhone, regardless of whether you recently purchased an iPhone 15 or an earlier model of Apple's well-known phone. We walk you through the process in our iPhone beginner's guide, starting with "Hello," and provide user manuals for some of Apple's in-built applications, including Messages, FaceTime, Mail, and more.

Also, find out how to download applications, games, movies, music, and more directly to your iPhone. This guide's purpose is to make setting up your new iPhone as simple as possible so you may customize it to its full potential.

You now own a brand-new iPhone. What follows? It might be difficult to set up the gadget for a first-time user. Numerous elements need to be taken into account, including network settings, night shift configuration, and Siri voice command setup. The feature set of the iPhone is fairly diverse. We created this lesson on the iPhone for beginners in 10 simple stages because of this.

Additionally, you must take extra effort to comprehend and adjust to the differences in the operating system if you transition from an Android to an iPhone. It's important to note that Android cellphones differ from one another more than iPhones do. Additionally, there are a number of new features you may benefit from when installing iOS 17 for the first time if you currently own an iPhone but are not using the most recent version.

Your brand-new iPhone is prepared for setup right out of the box. You'll be welcomed with a warm "Hello." You may then transfer your data from another phone, even an Android phone, or set up your iPhone as if it were completely new. It's quite difficult to make a mistake throughout the setup process as long as you carefully read each page, however you can always go back a page if you clicked the wrong choice.

CHAPTER 1: SETUP AND BASICS

Do you have a working knowledge of iPhone operation? When you first pick up an iPhone, it might be challenging to figure out how to operate it, especially if you're used to using an Android or a basic feature phone. Let me walk you through the fundamentals of operating an iPhone, including how to switch it on and off as well as how to make calls, send texts, and use applications.

The setup process is essentially the same regardless of which one of the several iPhones in Apple's portfolio you purchased. Here's how to become familiar with it so that you may live happily for, say, two to four years. Or only one, if you update every year. Being ready always makes things go more easily, so have the following things ready for the simplest setup possible:

- Your Wi-Fi details
- Your old phone (not essential, but it's smart to have it handy)
- Your SIM card (not required for eSIM activation)
- Your Apple account details (you must have an Apple account to use an iPhone)

Back up your old phone first. This will make copying your info over if it's an iPhone a little bit simpler. The quickest way to backup to iCloud is to go to Settings, press on your name up top, select iCloud, iCloud Backup, and then tap Back Up Now.
Make sure to download the Move to iOS Android app from Google Play if you're switching from Android. Tap Move Data from Android on the Apps & Data page when setting up your new iPhone. Return to your Android phone, launch the app, press Continue, and then adhere to the on-screen directions. While you can't move everything, you can transfer your email accounts, contacts, messages, images, and videos. Even some apps will transition. Just be aware that it can take a while for the data to travel, depending on how much there is.

TURN ON AND SET UP IPHONE
Holding down the power button will switch on your new iPhone after inserting your SIM card (if you are using an eSIM, skip this step). The Apple logo and the word "Hello" in many languages will welcome you. The next option is Quick Start, which is straightforward, or Set Up Manually, which is challenging. Whether this is your first iPhone will determine the route you choose.

Try Quick Start for the quickest way to set up your new iPhone if you are an Apple veteran and have your old iPhone on available. Simply bring your new iPhone close to your old one and confirm that you wish to use the same Apple ID on the new device after making sure your old iPhone is fully charged and that Bluetooth is switched on. Your new device should display an animation; use your old one to hover over it until the image shows in your viewfinder. On your old iPhone, wait until you see Finish on New [Device]. You may now set up Face ID by entering your password at the popup. The settings you wish to keep over, including those for your Apple Watch, if you have one, may then be selected. You can then specify what you want to back up in detail.

Alternately, you may just choose Other Options and choose to restore data from an iCloud backup or a Mac or PC backup. After entering your Apple ID and password, your iPhone will restart with all of your settings, preferences, applications, and more in place. In the meantime, go have a peppermint mocha. In other words, it will function just like your current gadget.

SET UP MANUALLY
Choose Set Up Manually if you're new to Apple, want a fresh start, or just like to fiddle with menu. To activate your iPhone or iPad, adhere to the onscreen directions. Set up a six-digit passcode, activate your eSIM or physical SIM in the new device, activate Face ID or Touch ID, recover or transfer your data and applications, and connect to your Wi-Fi network.

WAKE AND UNLOCK
You can wake an iPhone by hitting the side button or the Sleep/Wake button, depending on the model.

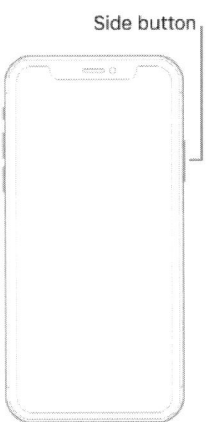

SET UP CELLULAR SERVICE
You are prompted to activate your iPhone with a cellular service provider as part of the initial iPhone Setup process. You may complete the iPhone cellular service setup in a matter of minutes as long as you have a SIM card or eSIM that has been activated for your cellular carrier's service plan. Push in toward the iPhone to eject the SIM tray by inserting a paper clip or SIM eject tool through the SIM tray's tiny hole.

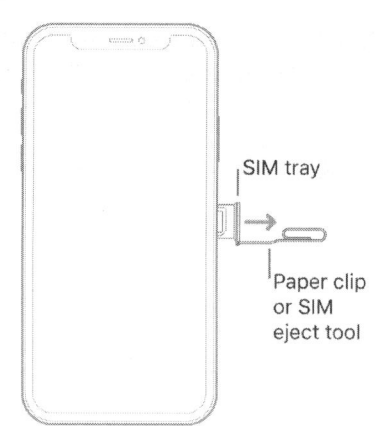

Put the nano-SIM in the tray and then put the iPhone back together. Depending on the iPhone model and your location, the SIM tray will have a different shape and position.

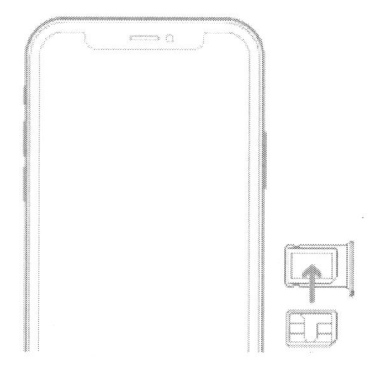

Use Wi-Fi or make sure you have cellular coverage.
If you have a contract, activate your iPhone through your carrier. If not, join a Wi-Fi network to complete the remaining setup steps.

Connect to the internet

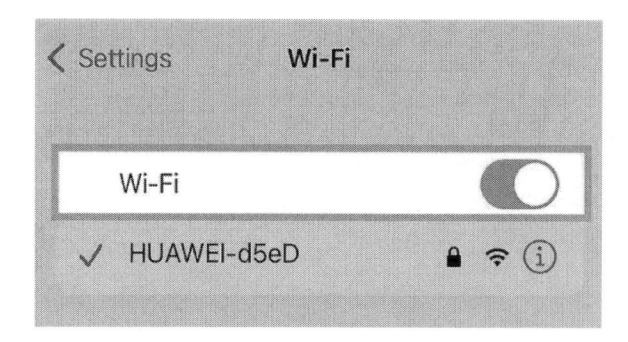

APPLE ID AND ICLOUD

You must first register an Apple ID account in order to utilize your iPhone and many of its functions. Use your main email address or any other email address.
Afterward, log in with your Apple ID. Enter your current Apple ID here if you have already used it with an Apple product.

Otherwise, you'll need to make one. Choose "Forgot password or don't have an Apple ID?" and then adhere to the on-screen instructions. To create your account, you'll need to provide details like your name, birthdate, and email address.

Setting up additional, optional services is one of the last tasks. You may click past these by choosing Set Up Later under Settings if you don't want to complete them right now (or ever).

Note: The applications chapter of this book contains an explanation of these processes.

These services include:
Apple Pay: In shops that accept them, add credit and debit cards to enable wireless payments.
Automatic Updates: Your phone will automatically download and install iOS and app updates if you enable this.
Developer Sharing: By sharing part of your usage information with developers, this feature enables them to provide better services.
iCloud: You may use Apple Music, the iCloud Keychain password manager, backups, and other features by using iCloud.
Location Services: By turning it on, applications like Find My iPhone and Apple Maps will be able to view and utilize your position.
Screen Time: With Apple's parental control feature, you may impose app restrictions and time restrictions on when the device is used.
Siri: By activating Siri, you can utilize voice control using Apple's virtual assistant. In this stage, you'll select a voice for Siri to learn and then teach it your own.

CHAPTER 2: PERSONALIZE YOUR IPHONE

Software personalization and customization may be challenging, especially if they are tucked away in menus that the majority of users never use. Apple, on the other hand, has adopted a distinctive strategy by allowing user customisation.

CHANGE SOUNDS AND VIBRATIONS

Change the sound that your iPhone makes when you receive a call, text, voicemail, email, reminder, or any kind of notification by going to Settings.

On compatible models, some activities, such touching and holding the Camera icon on the Home Screen, result in a tap, or haptic feedback.

TURN VIBRATION ON OR OFF ON YOUR IPHONE

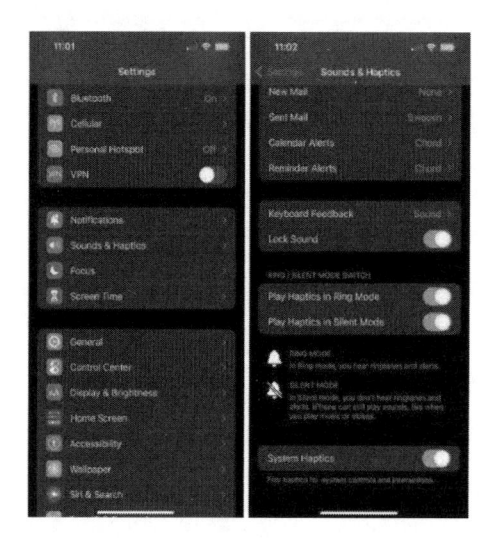

On iPhones, vibration corresponds to three functions: typing, the Ring/Silent (also known as mute) switch, and system operations in general. Through the Settings > Sounds and Haptics menu, you must customize one or more of them to your taste.

When the Ring switch is on, scroll down and enable Play Haptics in Ring Mode to change vibrations for notifications, etc. Play Haptics in Silent Mode is an option that you may turn off, but we strongly advise doing so as you won't receive notifications unless you are looking straight at your iPhone.

You can adjust the Haptic toggle by tapping Keyboard Feedback while typing.

By switching System Haptics, you may activate vibrations for "system controls and interactions," as Apple puts it.

HOW TO CREATE CUSTOM VIBRATION PATTERN

The Settings section on the iPhone conceals the option to design unique vibrating patterns. Here's how to access and modify your iPhone's unique vibration pattern.

Open Settings on iPhone.

Go to the Sounds & Haptics menu.

Choose the alert type you wish to alter, and then choose a unique vibrating pattern. We'll utilize ringtone in this case.

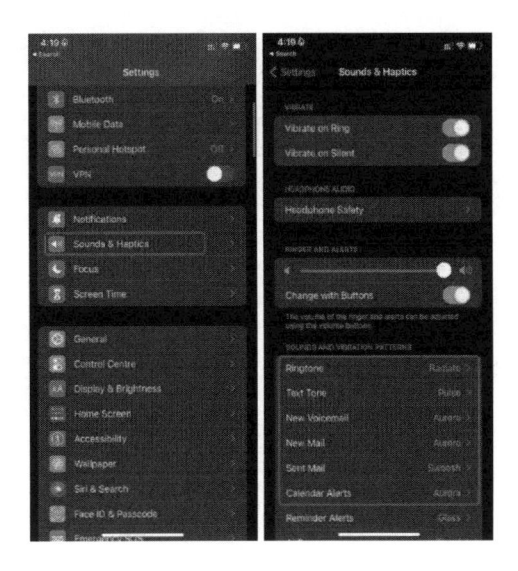

Tap on Vibration.
iOS's default vibration setting is taken from the Standard menu. You may select Create New Vibration from the Custom menu.

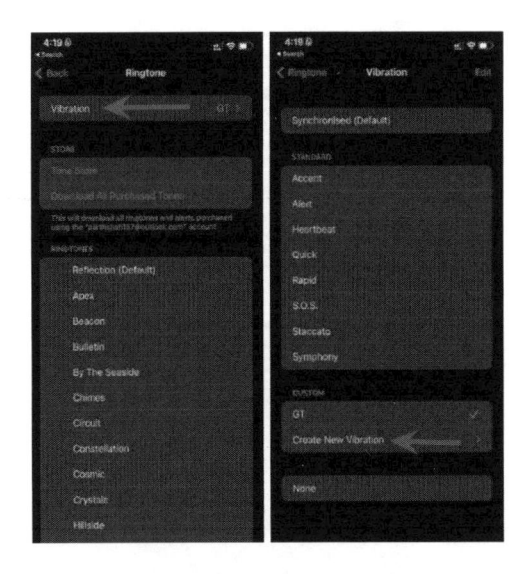

The New Vibration menu will appear. The blank screen will begin vibrating as soon as you tap it.
You may tap the screen repeatedly to make it vibrate continuously, raise your finger to pause it, and design your own vibrating pattern.
You may see the live preview at the bottom after creating a vibration pattern.
Press Play to take a peek at the generated vibration pattern.

Select the Save icon at the top after you are happy with the vibration pattern.
After naming it, click the Save button.

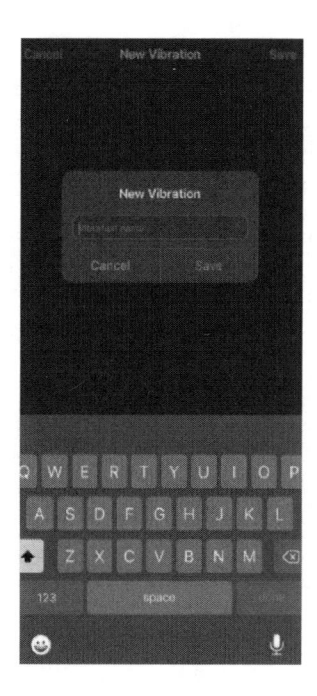

CREATE A CUSTOM LOCK SCREEN

Since the release of iOS 16, Apple has completely redesigned the iOS Lock Screen, making it more individualized than ever and able to show widgets with a wealth of information.

With iOS 17, you may add distinctive fonts, colors, and, for the first time, widgets to the Lock Screen. Simply unlock your iPhone using Face ID or Touch ID to get started, and then long-press the lock screen to access the Lock Screen gallery.

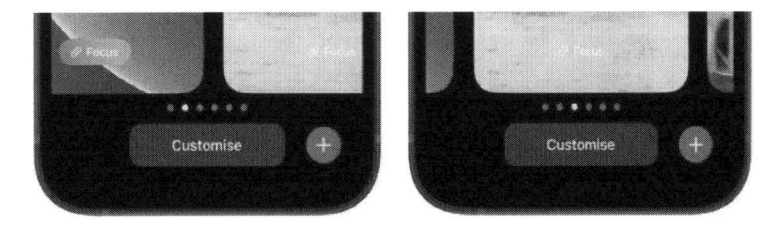

Alternatively, you may press Customize to make the Lock Screen you've chosen your own, or you can tap the blue + button to make a brand-new Lock Screen. Here, we'll concentrate on modifying an already-existing Lock Screen.
When you tap Customize, an interactive representation of your Lock Screen appears with several options available depending on the kind of Lock Screen. If you're designing a "Color" Lock Screen, you may swipe left and right to apply various styles to the image as well as press the colored circle on the left to modify the color and hue.

The bottom choices allow you to pick a different image from your photo library, apply a filter, and activate or disable the Perspective Zoom/Depth Effect if you're designing a "Photo" Lock Screen.
You should take note that the filters you may apply by swiping left and right are intelligently and automatically produced for the selected image, so you'll see various alternatives here depending on, for example, if it's a depth photo or a Color wallpaper. (If it's a photo, keep in mind that using different filters may also result in the time and date being shown in a different typeface.) The customization choices at

the bottom of the screen are more constrained if you're using a Lock Screen from one of Apple's "Collections."

You may add widgets above the time for additional time zones, a programmed alarm, the following event on the calendar, the weather, your activity rings, the following reminder, and a particular stock. The device's battery level, the calendar, the clock, the fitness tracker, the home screen, the news feed, the stock market, the weather, and other information-rich widgets can all be added below the time.

HOW TO CHANGE YOUR IPHONE WALLPAPER

Go to Settings > Wallpaper and touch the Add New Wallpaper option to add a new wallpaper design. The plus (+) symbol may also be accessed by long-pressing the screen when your phone is in lock screen mode. You'll notice a variety of alternatives for your wallpaper's decor.

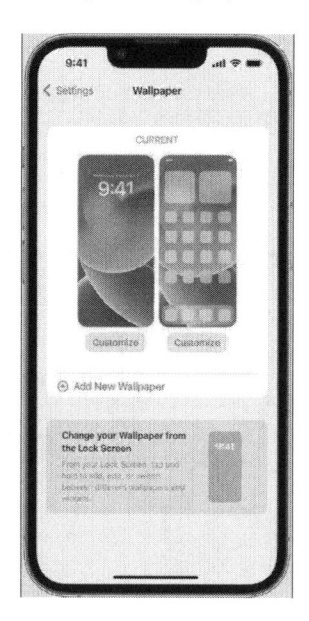

You may add various sorts of content using the icons at the top of the screen. Open your picture library by tapping the Photos button, then choose the image you wish to use, and hit Add.

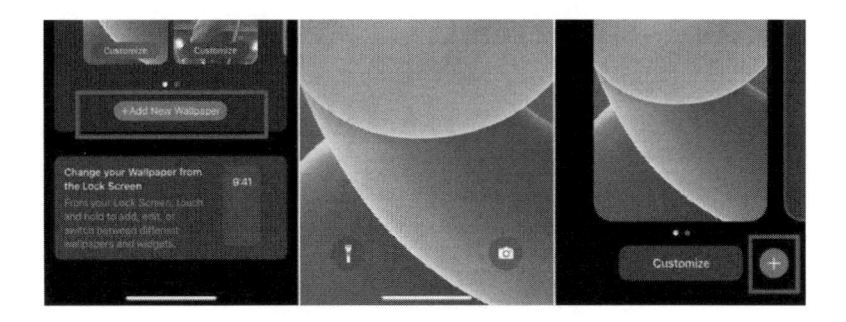

When choosing wallpaper for your Lock screen and Home screen, you'll be asked if you want to utilize the same image on both screens. Tap Set as Wallpaper Pair if you decide to. If not, choose an alternative design for your Home screen by tapping Customize Home screen.

Tap Photo Shuffle to add more than one picture. A smart photo collection, such as one for People or Places, may now be added. Otherwise, hit Choose Photos Manually to manually select the pictures you wish to use. After choosing each image you wish to use, press Add.

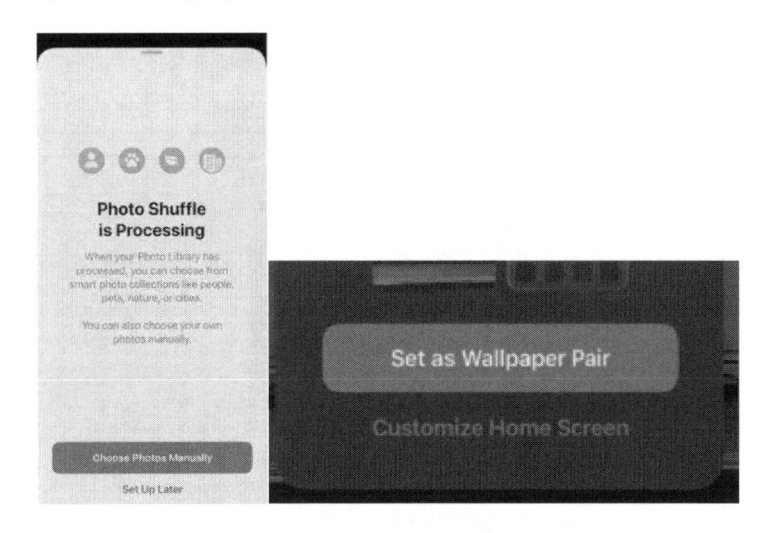

Choose Daily, Hourly, On Lock, or On Tap from the list of intervals available by tapping the ellipsis symbol on the preview screen. Select whether you want to match the background or separate Home screen customization after tapping Add again.

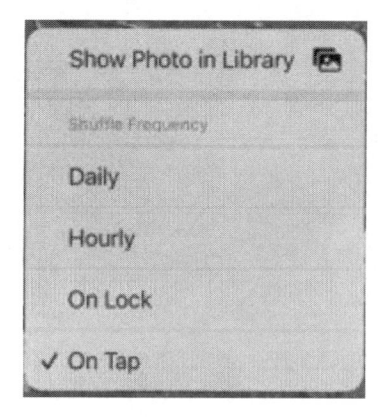

Select an emoji from one or more categories by tapping Emoji. You may select up to six. When finished, tap Add to add the images as a pair or separately edit the Home screen.

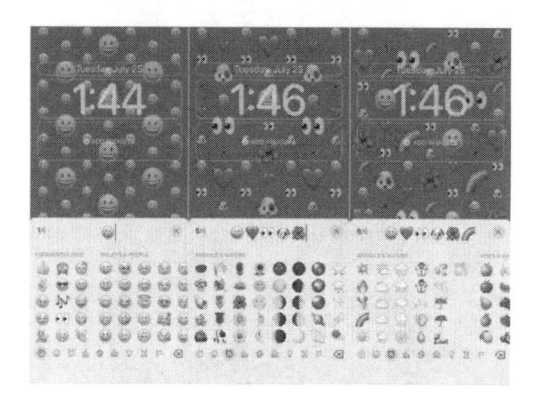

How to Quickly Set a Photo as Your Wallpaper
Select a photo by using the Photos app. Select the Use as Wallpaper option when you tap the Share icon. The image may then be cropped with a squeeze and other effects can be tried with a swipe. Tap Done when you're done.

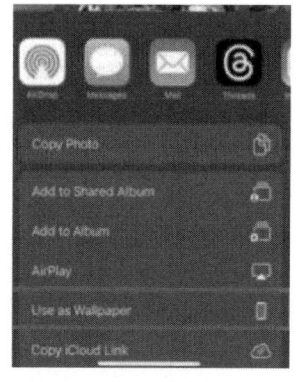

To utilize the image on both the Lock screen and the Home screen, select Set as Wallpaper to Pair. If not, choose modify Home Screen to individually modify the Home screen.

SCREEN BRIGHTNESS AND COLOR BALANCE

If you use an iPhone, you probably already know that your phone's display brightness will change automatically based on the quantity of ambient light. Although it's a helpful feature that ought to reduce eyestrain and make your screen easier to view, that isn't always the case.

The issue may be that even when you're outside in the sun, your display automatically dims. It may be challenging to see what's there if you're partially in the shadow since your phone may deceive it into automatically darkening the screen even when it doesn't have to. Because of auto-brightness, if you manually increase the brightness, it will just decrease once more.

DISABLE AUTO-BRIGHTNESS

The first thing you need do is to make sure that automatic brightness is turned off in your settings, which may seem a little apparent. It goes without saying that the function automatically changes your brightness based on the ambient light. However, you must turn off this function if you want to stop your display from constantly attempting to adapt.

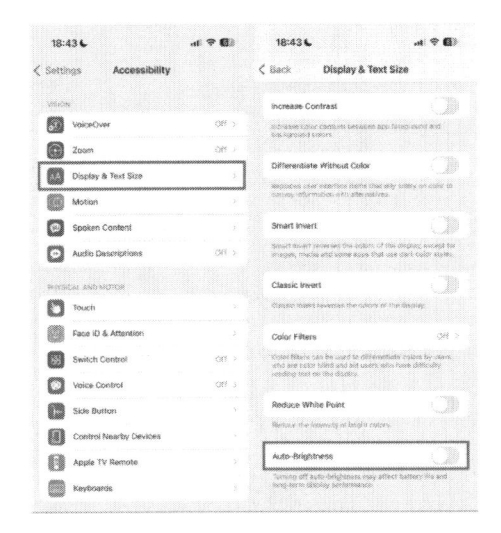

Toggle off Auto-Brightness at the bottom of the page under Accessibility > Display & Text Size in the Settings program. Since auto-brightness is hidden under Accessibility while you would believe it would be in Display & Brightness, it happens frequently that it gets turned on without you realizing it.

HOW TO ADJUST THE SCREEN ON TIME ON IPHONE

Finding the screen time-out option on an iPhone may be challenging, especially if you're transferring from an Android device. You'll find the options Turn off screen after or Sleep on Android. This has a different name on Apple: Auto-Lock.

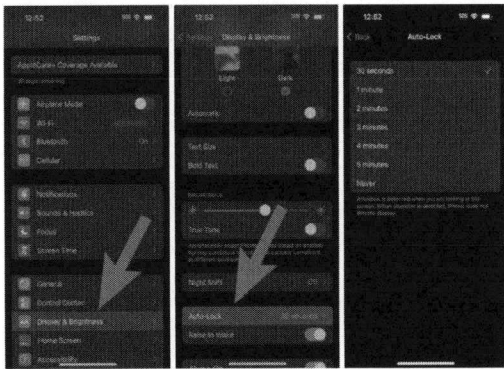

Navigate to Settings on your iPhone.

Tap Display & Brightness in Settings.
Click Auto-Lock.
Choose from the choices in the Auto-Lock menu 30 seconds, 1 minute, 2 minutes, 3 minutes, 4 minutes, 5 minutes, or Never.

HOW TO MAGNIFY YOUR SCREEN

To open the Settings app, tap the Settings icon on your Home screen. Tap Accessibility after scrolling down.

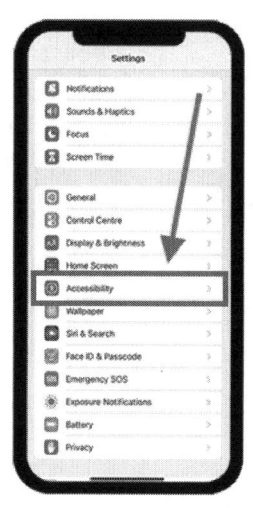

Tap Zoom on the Accessibility screen.

Tap the Zoom toggle switch to activate it on the Zoom screen.

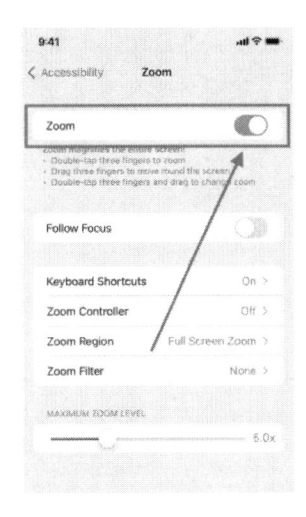

Zoom offers two options for screen magnification. Full Screen Zoom, which enlarges the whole screen, and Window Zoom, a movable window that enlarges the space beneath it.

Select Zoom Region. Select between Full Screen Zoom and Window Zoom on the next screen.

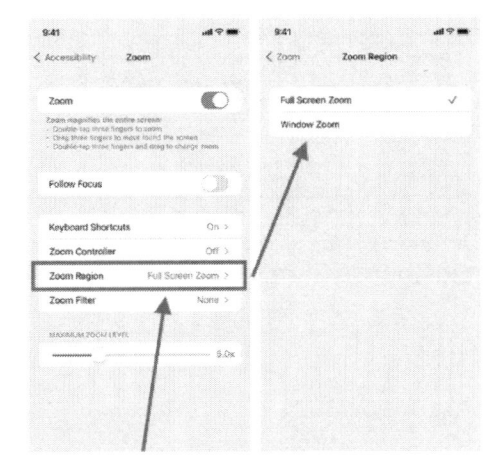

Zoom may leap to the text entry point and continue to follow you as you type by using the Follow Focus feature. Toggle Follow Focus on by tapping the toggle.

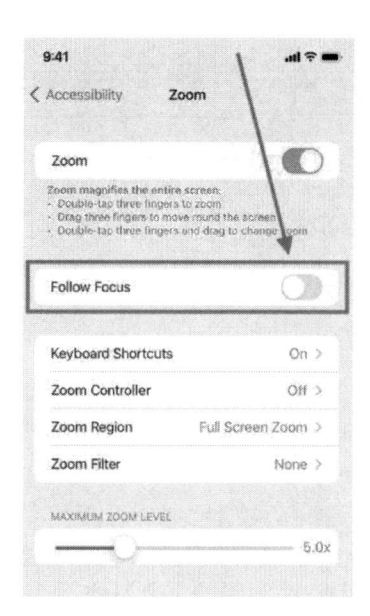

It might be challenging to type when the entire screen is large. When a keyboard appears, Smart Typing activates Window mode and just enlarges the text. Toggle Smart Typing on by tapping the toggle switch.

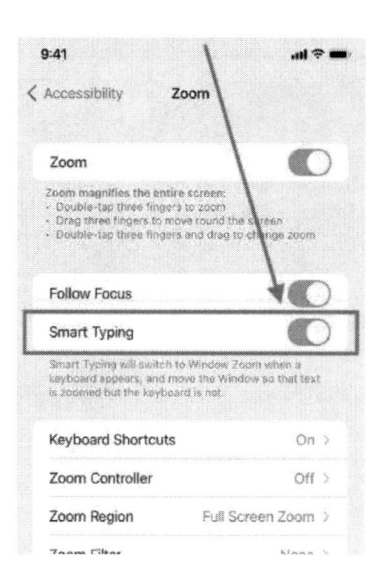

CHANGE THE COLOUR OF THE ZOOM CONTROLLER
By default, the Zoom Controller is black and white. You can change the white parts to another colour to make it easier to see. Tap Colour and choose from the colour options on the next screen.

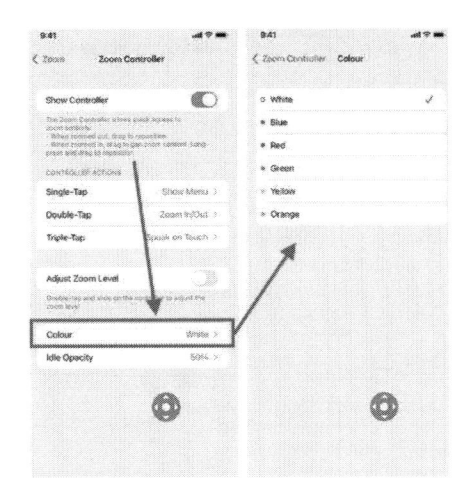

CHANGE THE NAME OF YOUR IPHONE

We have the solutions you need, whether you want to customize your phone or simply want to make it simpler to identify.
To rename your iPhone, follow the instructions below.
Select Settings.
Click General.

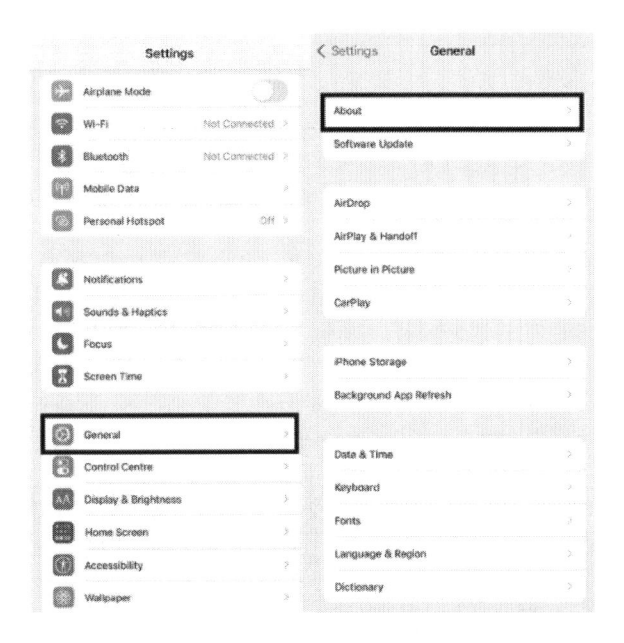

Click About.
Select Name.

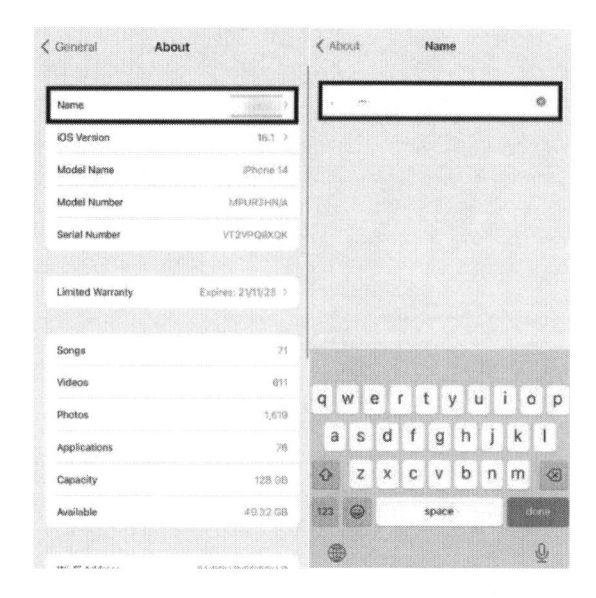

Modify the name. Delete the existing name and replace it with the one you desire. Once you're finished, press Back to save your modifications.
Repeat the preceding procedures to examine your smartphone's current name to see whether the name has changed. You may also try using your phone's hotspot or Airdrop feature, then check to see whether its name displays on any open connections with other devices.

CHANGE THE DATE AND TIME

Although your iPhone should automatically display the proper time, this isn't always the case. Fortunately, changing the time and date under the Settings is simple. If you don't want to miss any more crucial meetings, you may even do this to have your iPhone start up a few minutes earlier.

HOW TO CHANGE TIME ON YOUR IPHONE AUTOMATICALLY

When you purchase a new iPhone, the time setting is by default configured to update automatically to show the right time for your location. However, there may be times when you need to explicitly enable this feature. Here is how to go about it:
Open the Settings app on your iPhone after unlocking it.
Tap the "General" tab after scrolling down. To access the next menu, press the "Date & Time" tab now.

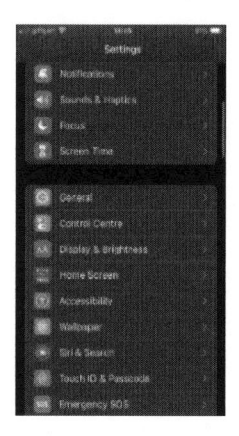

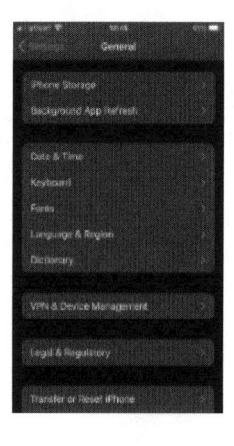

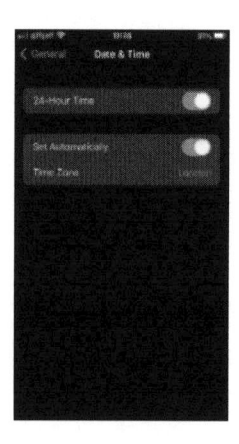

Now, if it hasn't already, enable the "Set Automatically" toggle.
And it's finished. This is how to set your iPhone to automatically adjust the time. But if the issue continues, it's conceivable that your iPhone's time zone setting is incorrect.

CHANGE TIME ZONE ON IPHONE AUTOMATICALLY

Your iPhone must be able to recognize the time zone you're in in order to guarantee that it always shows the proper time. Here's how to set your iPhone to automatically change time zones.
Go to the "Privacy & Security" option in the Settings app on your iPhone.

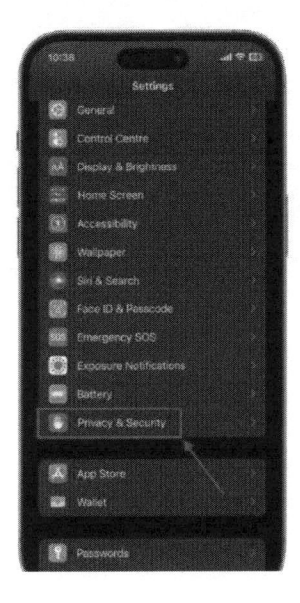

If the Location Services option is not already selected, tap on "Location Services" under the Privacy & Security options and change it to "On".

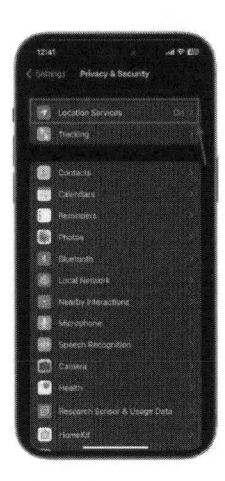

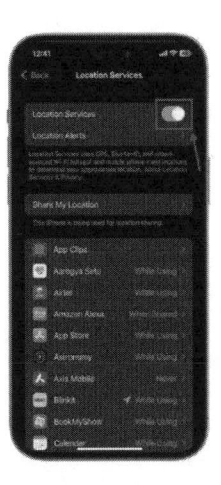

Scroll down until you see "System Services" on the menu. Click or tap it to get a list of the system services that are using the location service.

Ensure that the "Setting Time Zone" toggle is turned on on the System Services settings screen. Turn it on if it is currently off. The "Date & Time" settings will now display the chosen time zone, and it will update automatically.

How to Change Time on Your iPhone Manually
If you have followed the following instructions but your iPhone still cannot show the time correctly. You are left with no choice except to manually set the time in that situation. Here is how to go about it.
Scroll down in the Settings app and select the "General" option. Next, select "Date & Time" to modify your iPhone's time settings.

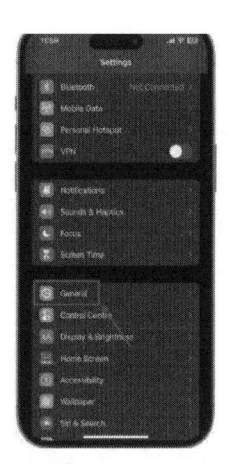

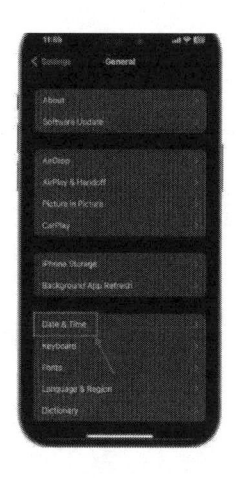

Here, toggle off the "Set Automatically" setting.

To choose the precise time zone for your present location, hit the "Time Zone" option now.

To manually set the day and time that will appear on your iPhone, touch "Date" and "Time" after that.

CHANGE THE LANGUAGE AND REGION
On the iPhone, switching between Chinese, Arabic, Spanish, and a variety of other languages is really simple. The steps to changing the language and region on an iPhone are listed below.

HOW TO CHANGE LANGUAGE ON IPHONE
Select General under Settings.
Click on Language & Region.
Select Add Language.
Select a language.

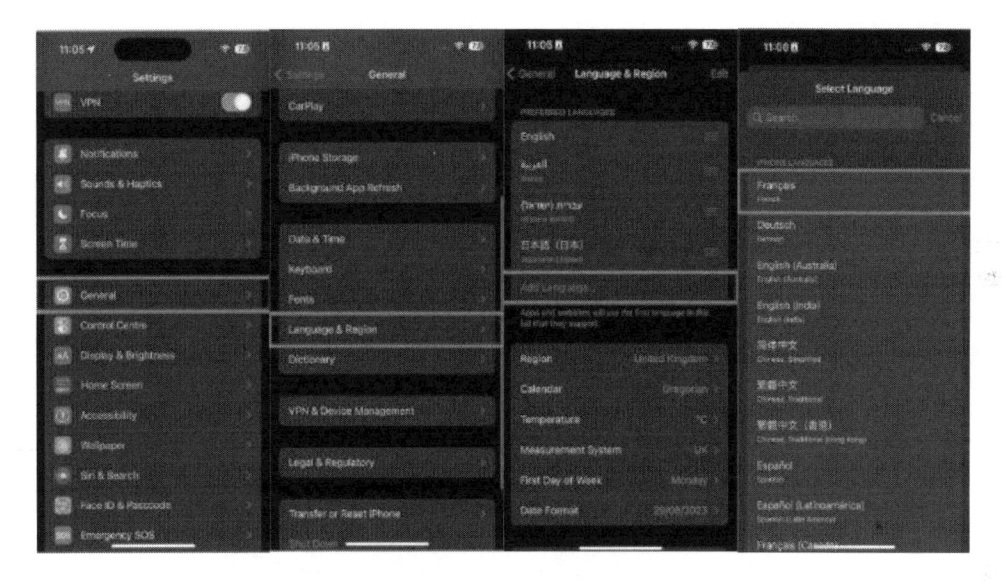

Click Use. Your iPhone's default language will now be this one.

HOW TO CHANGE REGION ON IPHONE
Select Settings > General > Language & Region > Region from the menu. Choose your region on the Region page, then hit Done.

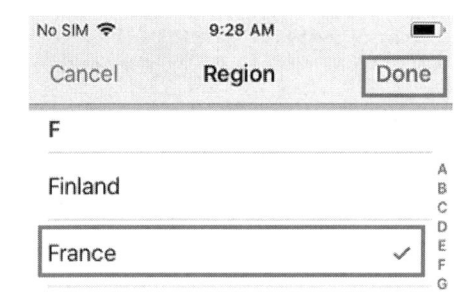

To finish the procedure, click OK on the Confirmation pop-up.
You will be requested to change your language if you switch to a region with a different language. If you'd rather not switch languages, hit Cancel instead of choosing the language you want to use.
The display of currency and temperature on your iPhone may vary if you change the region.

SET UP FOCUS, NOTIFICATIONS, AND DO NOT DISTURB
Since the release of iOS 15, Apple has included Focus modes to aid in task retention. The purpose of this filtering was to prevent apps or alerts that you don't want to appear at certain times from interrupting your "in-the-moment" experience. Apple has also included a few fresh choices in iOS 17 to speed up the procedure. This includes the option to combine Focus modes with lock screens and watchfaces, as well as the ability to turn off alerts from particular applications or persons.

Setting up Focus might be a little intimidating at first. There are several options and modifications that may be made. In fact, it could take some time before you find the settings that best suit your way of living. But in the end, it will be worthwhile since you won't be distracted when you need to focus and you won't be plagued by pointless alerts when you have other things to do.

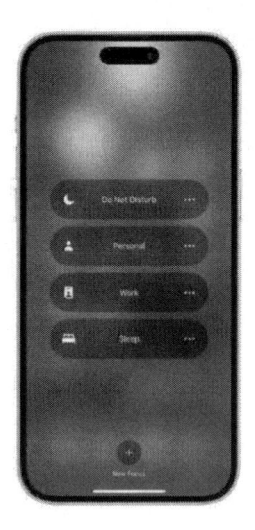

SETUP DO NOT DISTURB
A number of submenus that are intended to assist you identify the people and applications that are permitted to send alerts while the mode is on are the first thing you see when you get on the Do Not Disturb focus page. Following that, you'll notice choices for customizing displays, a choice to switch the mode on and off automatically at specified times, and Focus Filters that enable you alter how applications behave in a particular Focus.

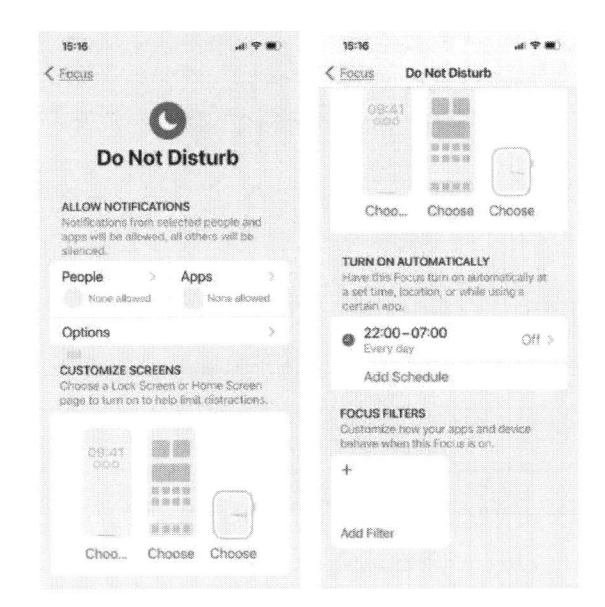

HOW TO ALLOW NOTIFICATIONS

You may choose in Focus which applications or people you want to get notifications from even when Do Not Disturb is turned on. You could wish to permit calls from family members or Slack alerts from work, for instance. You may now turn off alerts from particular persons or applications in iOS 17. Keep in mind that all of your devices must be running the most recent software if you wish to apply this approach on all of them.

Tap on the People or Apps boxes to access the Notifications pane and set these exceptions.

On your iPhone, go to Settings -> Focus -> Do Not Disturb to get the "Do Not Disturb" focus mode screen. Click or press the "People" tab located in the left corner of the screen.

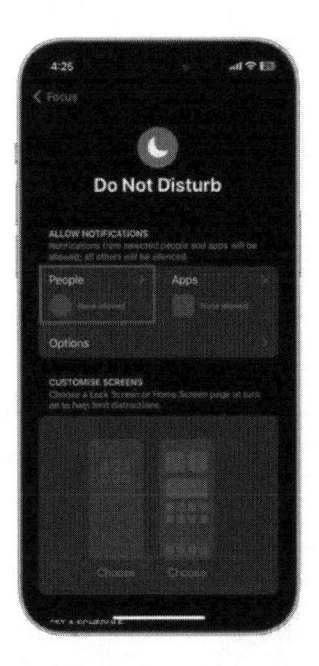

The next page will present you with two choices: "Silence Notifications From" and "Allow Notifications From."

To silence all alerts from a particular contact, select the "Silence Notifications From" option. Turn on the "Allow Calls from Silenced People" toggle to only receive calls and not alerts from the selected contacts.

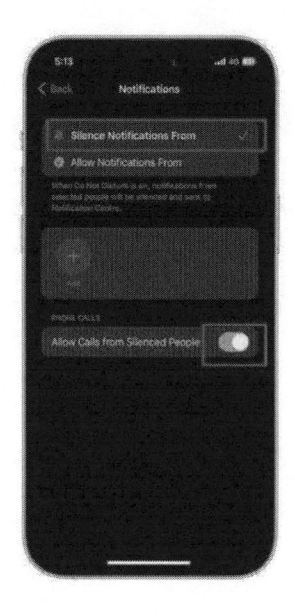

To add contacts to a list of persons whose alerts you want to quiet while Do Not Disturb mode is enabled, tap the "+" symbol.

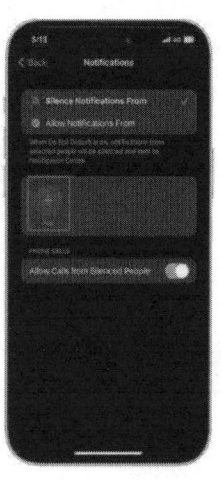

Alternatively, while using Do Not Disturb on your iPhone, choose "Allow Notifications From" to get alerts from certain contacts.

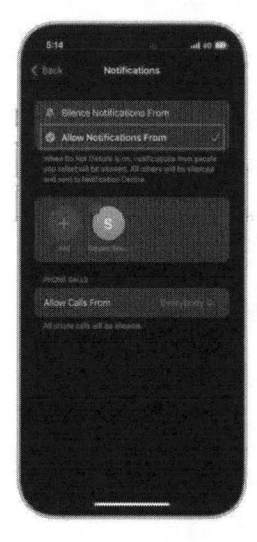

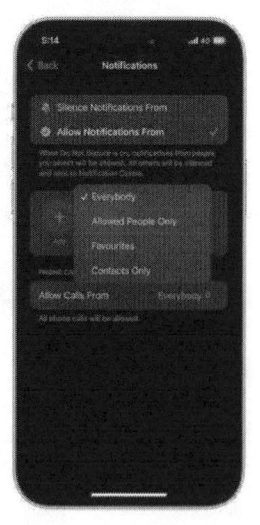

By selecting an option from the list that displays after hitting the "Allow Calls From" button under this option, you may also accept calls from particular individuals.

CUSTOMIZE FOCUS FILTERS

In the Do Not Disturb focus mode, you may also install Focus Filters, such as App Filters and System Filters. In the event that a focus mode is activated, these filters let you change system and in-app settings. Focus Filters provide you fine-grained control over various focus settings. When the Do Not Disturb mode is activated, app filters let you adjust specific apps, whereas system filters let you customize settings generally. To apply Focus Filters, follow to the steps outlined below:
On your iPhone, open the Do Not Disturb settings menu and scroll down until you see the "Focus Filters" choice. Click the "Add Filter" button now.

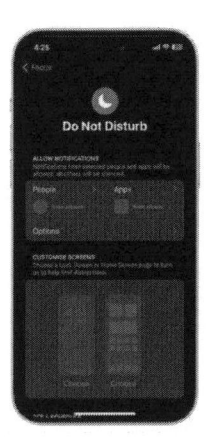

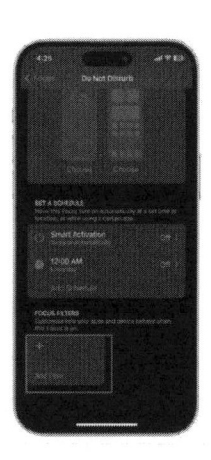

Two parts may be found here: one for "App Filters" and one for "System Filters."

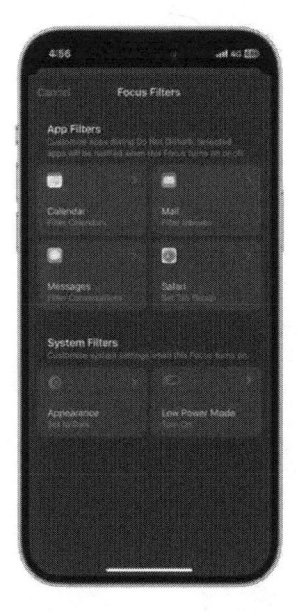

There are four applications you may add under the App Filters. Filters for Do Not Disturb mode -
Calendar: Choosing which calendar to display at what time.
Setting mail focus filters
Allow or disallow alerts of messages from certain individuals.
Safari: To permit the use of a certain tab group when the Do Not Disturb mode is activated.
You can choose from the next two choices under the System Filters section.

When the Do Not Disturb mode is on, the look may be set to dark or light.
Low Power Mode: With Do Not Disturb mode, automatically enable or disable low power mode.

How to Enable Do Not Disturb from the Lock Screen

With iOS 16, you can now add widgets to the iPhone lock screen and personalize its appearance. Multiple lock screens with various home screens and backgrounds are now possible to configure. Although many users are already aware of this, some may not be aware that they may associate a certain lock screen with the "Do Not Disturb" focus mode. This implies that whenever a user changes the iPhone's lock screen, the Do Not Disturb mode will immediately activate. We have shown how to connect Do Not Disturb mode to a specific lock screen here:

Long-press the lock screen on your unlocked iPhone to access the lock screen editing mode.
Select "Focus" by tapping on the symbol in the bottom-center of the screen.

The focus modes list will then display in a new "Link Focus" pop-up window. To connect this concentration mode with the active lock screen, tap "Do Not Disturb." When you press the "X" in the upper right corner, a Do Not Disturb symbol will appear at the bottom of your screen. This shows that the lock screen and the Do Not Disturb mode have been connected.

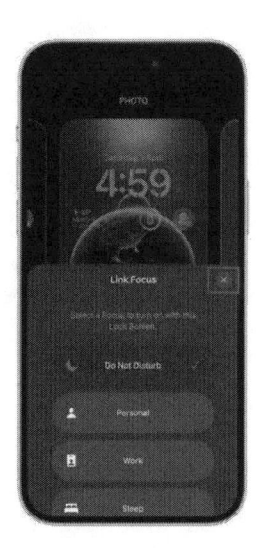

CHAPTER 3: EVERYTHING ABOUT THE LATEST IPHONE 15

This chapter will assist you in getting the most out of your iPhone 15, regardless of whether you're upgrading from an earlier iPhone or are entirely new to the devices.

IPHONE 15-SERIES PRICE

Here are the new iPhones' pricing from Apple. If you want an iPhone that is not network-locked, you will have to pay extra for it in the United States. These costs are for unlocked iPhones in the United Kingdom. These costs are sometimes more affordable than their 2022 equivalents. The price of the iPhone 14 and iPhone 14 Plus increased in 2022, and the Pro and Pro Max's price remained constant in the United States, decreased in the United Kingdom, and increased in Australia.

Additionally, the 15 Pro Max now has 256GB of storage as standard, as opposed to 128GB, so it isn't as pricey as it would appear.

iPhone 15	**128GB:** $799 / £799 / AU$1,499 **256GB:** $899 / £899 / AU$1,699 **512GB:** $1,099 / £1,099 / AU$2,049	**128GB:** $829 / £849 / AUD$1,399 **256GB:** $929 / £959 / AUD$1,579 **512GB:** $1,129 / £1,179 / AUD$1,899
iPhone 15 Plus	**128GB:** $899 / £899 / AU$1,649 **256GB:** $999 / £999 / AU$1,849 **512GB:** $1,199 / £1,199 / AU$2,199	**128GB:** $929 / £949 / AUD$1,579 **256GB:** $1,029 / £1,059 / AUD$1,749 **512GB:** $1,229 / £1,279 / AUD$2,099
iPhone 15 Pro	**128GB:** $999 / £999 / AU$1,849 **256GB:** $1,099 / £1,099 / AU$2,049 **512GB:** $1,299 / £1,299 / AU$2,399 **1TB:** $1,499 / £1,499 / AU$2,749	**128GB:** $999 / £1,099 / AUD$1,699 **256GB:** $1,099 / £1,209 / AUD$1,869 **512GB:** $1,299 / £1,429 / AUD$2,219 **1TB:** $1,499 / £1,649 / AUD$2,569
iPhone 15 Pro Max	**256GB:** $1,199 / £1,199 / AU$2,199 **512GB:** $1,399 / £1,399 / AU$2,549 **1TB:** $1,599 / £1,599 / AU$2,899	**128GB:** $1,099 / £1,199 / AUD$1,899 **256GB:** $1,199 / £1,309 / AUD$2,099 **512GB:** $1,399 / £1,529 / AUD$2,419 **1TB:** $1,599 / £1,749 / AUD$2,769

IPHONE 15 AND USB-C

The four iPhones from 2023 each include a USB-C connector. Older iPhone models have not received an update. Only the Pro versions can handle 10Gbps data transfers at a quicker rate. Like Lightning, the iPhone 15 and iPhone 15 Plus have a 480Mbps speed limit.

There is a USB-C cable included in the package, but if you don't already have a 20W adaptor plug, you will need to purchase one.Considering that the new iPhone 15 series features a USB-C connector, you might be wondering how to charge one. Since 2020, there hasn't been a plug in the box, but you will discover a USB-C cable that, if you have a 20w plug, will enable rapid charging. The second choice is wireless charging.

iPhone 15Dynamic Island and How to Use It

Display pixels surrounding what Apple refers to as the "Dynamic Island" on the iPhone 14 Pro and all of this year's iPhone 15 models combine it into one pill-shaped area that changes size and shape to accommodate various types of alerts, notifications, and interactions, transforming it into a sort of front-and-center information hub.
Which iPhone Models Feature Dynamic Island?

The Dynamic Island on the iPhone 14 series is only available on the iPhone 14 Pro; the regular iPhone 14 devices have the same notch as the iPhone 13 models. Apple added Dynamic Island support for the iPhone 15, 15 Plus, 15 Pro, and 15 Pro Max in 2023.

Can I Interact With Dynamic Island?
You can interact with some of the stuff that is shown on the Dynamic Island. If it's displaying information on an app's background activities, for instance, you may press the Dynamic Island to jump right into the

relevant app. You may also long-press the Dynamic Island to display a widget with playback controls when the media is playing, for example.

The Dynamic Island may also show several background events simultaneously, such as when a timer is running out while music is playing. As a result, you can view and engage with both activities as the island divides into a bigger pill-shaped region and a smaller circular one. Similar to how you do with the default Dynamic Island interface, you can switch between them and tap into them.

EVERYTHING YOU NEED TO KNOW ABOUT 5X OPTICAL ZOOM OF IPHONE 15 PRO MAX

The iPhone 15 Pro Max from Apple has a tetraprism lens system that offers up to 5x optical zoom, which is an advance over the 3x zoom seen in the iPhone 15 Pro and the iPhone 14 from the previous generation.With a mix of optical image stabilization and an autofocus 3D sensor-shift module, the Telephoto lens on the iPhone 15 Pro Max has Apple's most sophisticated camera stabilization system ever.

According to Apple, the iPhone 15 Pro Max's Telephoto lens opens at /2.8 while shooting with 5x enabled, enabling outstanding light control. The 10x lens on the Galaxy S23 Ultra, in contrast, has an aperture of /4.9. A smaller aperture makes it possible for the camera's sensor to collect more light, which can be especially useful for images taken in Night mode.

Simply hit the 5x button at the bottom of the viewfinder to activate 5x optical zoom on the built-in Camera app. By pinching in the viewfinder while 5x optical zoom is activated, you can also zoom in up to 25x digitally. However, keep in mind that the more digitally you zoom in, the worse the image quality becomes.

The maximum digital zoom for the iPhone 15 Pro Max is 25x, which is still less than the competitors. In contrast to the Pixel 7 Pro, which boasts 30x digital "Super Res Zoom" with a 5x optical zoom lens, Samsung's most recent Galaxy S23 Ultra smartphone offers 100x Space Zoom and can shoot photographs up to 330 feet away.
To its credit, Apple has resisted using digital zoom because of its subpar quality. Digital zoom employs software augmentation to crop in whereas optical zoom uses the camera's hardware to provide a clean, sharp image. On the iPhone 15 Pro, which is only capable of 3x optical zoom, the 5x optical zoom function is exclusive to the iPhone 15 Pro Max.

Customize the Action button on iPhone 15 Pro and iPhone 15 Pro Max

Here are all the tasks that may be assigned to the Action Button so that it can be tailored to your requirements.
On your iPhone 15 Pro or iPhone 15 Pro Max, open the Settings app.
Tap on the Action Button option after scrolling down to find it.
When you do this, the Action Button settings page, which is unlike any other settings page on the iPhone in appearance, will open.

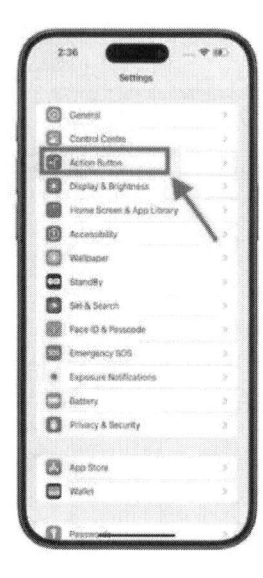

Swipe left or right to see the name and icon of the activities, which will make it easier for you to decide the action you want the Action Button to carry out.
No "Done" or "Okay" buttons are required to validate your choice. To begin using the new functionality, simply swipe to the relevant function and then return.
Some of the fundamental adjustments you can carry out with the brand-new action button on the iPhone 15 Pro and 15 Pro Max include turning on/off the flashlight, switching between ringing and quiet mode, accessing the voice memo app, and switching between Focus modes. The following is a detailed explanation of some further advanced activities you may carry out using the Action button:

Open a Camera Mode

Stop on the Camera option while sliding through the available choices, and an Up-Down arrow symbol will appear next to the Photos icon.
A pop-up menu with the camera options will show when you tap the Up-Down arrow. You have the choice of taking a photo, a selfie, a video, a portrait, or both.
Select your preferred camera mode, and the camera app will now launch in that mode each time you touch and hold the Action Button.

USE AS A SHORTCUT OR TO OPEN APPS

To begin, select the Shortcut option and then press the blue "Choose a Shortcut..." button.
When the Shortcuts app pops up, you may select the Shortcut you wish to use by pressing the Action Button.
Additionally, you may configure the Action Button to only start a certain program on this screen (using shortcuts).

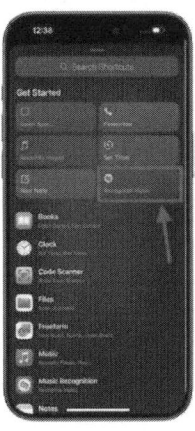

ACTIVATE AN ACCESSIBILITY FEATURE

Finally, on the Action option settings page, click the "Choose a feature..." option under Accessibility.
Accessibility settings like Classic Invert, Color Filters, Reduce Motion, Reduce White Point, and others are available for you to enable here.
You won't need to launch the Settings app each time you want to activate and modify accessibility features thanks to this method.

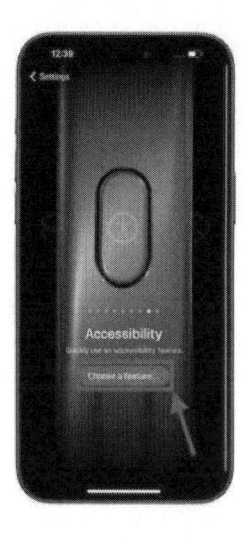

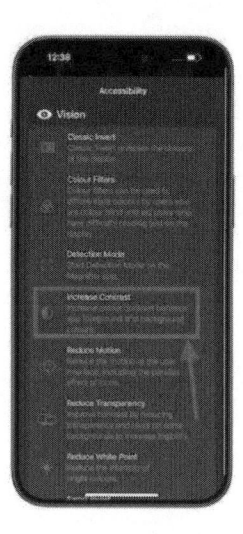

The end of that. The new Action Button on the iPhone 15 Pro and 15 Pro Max may be customized in this way.

IPHONE 15, PLUS, PRO, MAX NEW FEATURES

The new phones can perform a few tasks that their forerunners were unable to. For example, the addition of USB-C makes it slightly simpler to utilize a single charger for several Apple products. The Dynamic Island's features have been increased, and it is now available on all four models (instead of just the Pro handsets last year). The reverse charging feature, though, is arguably the most intriguing change. With it, you can now use your phone to charge an Apple Watch or a pair of 2nd-generation AirPods Pro.

The Pro versions include a ton of design improvements in addition to the brand-new, lightning-fast A17 Pro processor. They also have some really unique photographic capabilities.

The environmental arguments made by Apple are also important to note. The four iPhone 15 devices all make use of more recycled materials than earlier models. While the Pro models feature "100% recycled aluminum substructure and 100% recycled cobalt in the battery-both firsts for Apple," the standard models boast "100% recycled cobalt in the battery and 100 percent recycled copper in the main logic board, copper wire in the Taptic Engine, and copper foil in the inductive charger in MagSafe," along with impressive claims related to aluminum, gold, and rare earth materials.

The corporation also boasts of various energy efficiency successes, as well as the elimination or reduction of plastic and dangerous chemicals, and it has vowed to "no longer use leather in any new Apple products."

HOW TO TAKE PORTRAIT MODE PHOTOS ON IPHONE 15

Apple's Portrait Mode, which enables iPhone users to take photos with the subject in focus and the background blurred, has grown to be a popular method for capturing eye-catching pictures employing the depth-of-field effect known as bokeh.

Apple has enhanced its portrait game with the release of the iPhone 15 owing to an upgraded camera system that makes it simpler to snap photos with more information and offers better portrait performance in low light.

Additionally, iPhone 15 users may now shoot portrait photos without ever entering Portrait mode. Here is the procedure. Aim the camera toward a human, dog, or cat while the Camera app is active. Watch for a circle f symbol to show up in the viewfinder's lower left corner. Tap a topic in the viewfinder to concentrate on it if the icon doesn't show up. To make a yellow circle appear around the f icon, tap it.

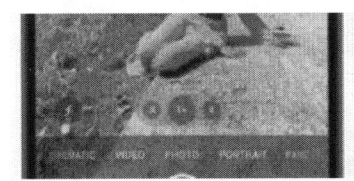

Tap the shutter button when you're prepared to shoot a picture with the Portrait effect.
All there is to it is that. You may now view your portrait photo simply touching on it in the Camera interface's corner.
You may convert a shot into a Portrait with depth information after the image has been captured thanks to the advanced Portrait mode, which is only available on iPhone 15 models.

How to Turn Photos into Portraits After Shooting on IPhone 15
When you take a picture of a human, a cat, or a dog on the iPhone 15, the camera recognizes them in the frame and automatically records rich depth information, allowing you to instantly or later in the Photos app create a breathtaking image.
Any shot taken in shot mode may be seen in fullscreen by tapping it in the Photos app. The top-left corner will display a Portrait button if depth information for the image is available.
To activate the depth of field effect, tap the Portrait button and choose Portrait from the dropdown menu.

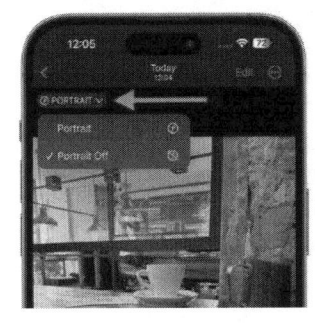

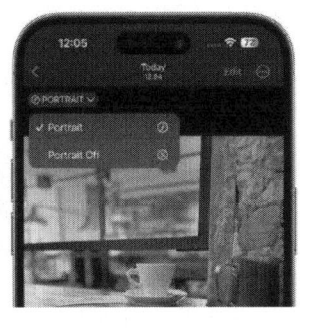

If you don't like the outcome, hit the Portrait button once again and choose Portrait Off to turn it off.

In photos, change the portrait effect
Any shot taken in shot mode may be seen in fullscreen by tapping it in the Photos app. A Portrait indicator will show up in the top-left corner of the image if depth information is available for it.
Click Edit.

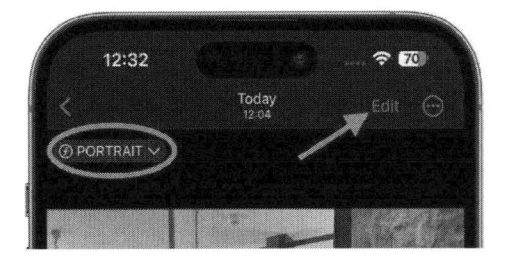

To activate the depth of field information, tap the Portrait button.
Increase or reduce the amount of background blur in the portrait using the Depth Control slider.

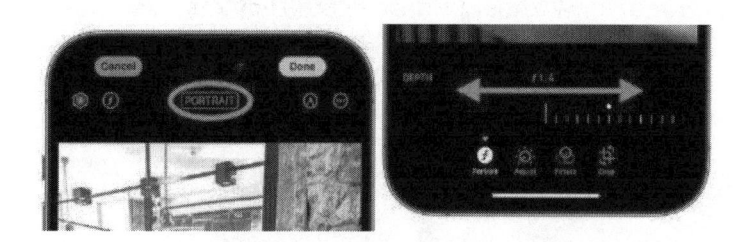

Simply tap the new topic to make it the image's focal point, and the emphasis will move to that area.

Tap Done to finish.

Simply open the picture again, choose Edit, and then select Revert to reverse any portrait effects.

HOW TO LOCATE FRIENDS WITH PRECISION FINDING ON IPHONE 15
If both you and your friend have an iPhone 15, you may find each other and meet up using Apple's Precision Finding function.Precision Finding for People was a feature that Apple added to iPhone 15 versions. With the use of on-screen instructions and distance information, Precision Finding may lead you directly to your buddy if both you and they have an iPhone 15 or iPhone 15 Pro model.

Follow these steps to use Precision Finding to locate your friend:
your iPhone's Find My app should be opened.
To meet a friend, touch People at the bottom of the screen, then tap their name. You might need to disclose your location or ask for their location if you aren't following each other.
Tap Directions to go closer to their location if you are not already there. If you're already close to your buddy, hit Find to let them know you're attempting to find them, then follow the on-screen prompts to obtain directions.

An arrow with an estimated distance from them will point in their direction once you are sufficiently close to one another. The screen will turn green if you are moving in the appropriate direction. Tap the Message icon in the bottom-right corner of the screen if you want to send the person you're looking for a message. Once you've located your buddy, click the X to complete by closing the window.

How to stop Your iPhone 15 Battery from Charging Beyond 80%

A new battery health setting that, when selected, prohibits the devices from charging over 80% at all times is available on all iPhone 15 and iPhone 15 Pro models.

The new setting is distinct from the current Optimized Battery Charging function on iPhones, which proactively postpones charging after 80% until a better time by observing how frequently the device is charged. The iPhone will never charge over 80% when the 80% hard limit is enabled.

Launch the Settings app.

Battery -> Battery Health & Charging can be tapped.

Select Optimize Charging.

To turn it on, tap the 80% Limit option. Select Optimised Battery Charging or None if necessary.

The 80% hard limit can lengthen the time an iPhone battery is fully charged, just like Optimized Battery Charging, which increases battery life.

HOW TO CHARGE APPLE WATCH, AIRPODS, OR ANOTHER IPHONE WITH YOUR IPHONE 15
Instead of using a Lightning port for charging and data transmission, Apple's iPhone 15 and iPhone 15 Pro models utilize a USB-C port. The new port also enables an iPhone 15 to directly charge AirPods or an Apple Watch. You no longer need to carry around a battery pack if your AirPods or Apple Watch run out of battery and you don't have access to a charger by using the battery of your iPhone.

Additionally, if you connect two iPhone 15s to one another, they talk to find out which one has the lesser battery and then transfer power accordingly. Therefore, you may put your iPhone into your friend's iPhone to charge it if your battery is low and their iPhone 15 has a full battery.

If you connect a USB-C Android phone to an iPhone with a lower battery level and the Android device supports USB juice Delivery, the Android device will be able to supply battery juice. Keep in mind that the results will be unpredictable if the Android phone lacks USB PD since there is no way to forecast which phone will be the charger and which will get the charge. It's a nice feature that wasn't possible with Lightning, but you'll need the proper cable, such as a USB-C to USB-C cable for the new AirPods Pro 2 USB-C Charging Case or a USB-C Apple Watch charging puck.

A 15-inch iPhone can only provide 4.5W of power when charging another device. While it is suitable for tiny gadgets like the Apple Watch, it won't supply enough power for an iPhone, thus when using the iPhone to iPhone charging functionality, expect slower charging times.

HOW TO CHECK BATTERY CYCLE COUNT ON iPHONE 15
A useful indicator to assess the battery health of your smartphone is the number of completed battery cycles, which Apple has made available on all iPhone 15 models.
Launch the Settings app.
Select About from General.
Examine the number next to Cycle Count in the "Battery" column by scrolling down.

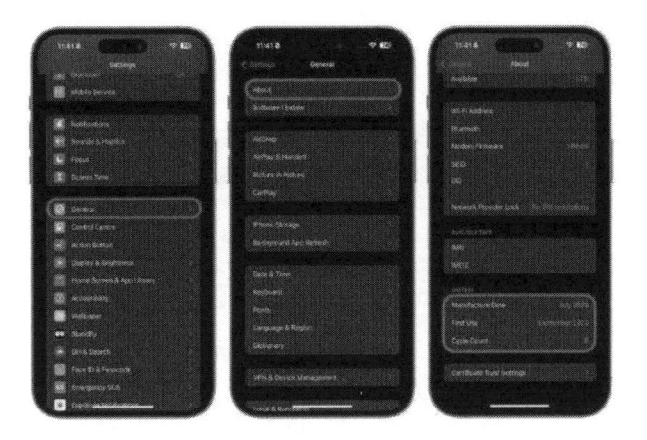

HOW TO HARD RESET THE iPHONE 15 (ALL MODELS)
Press and let go of the Volume Up button quickly.

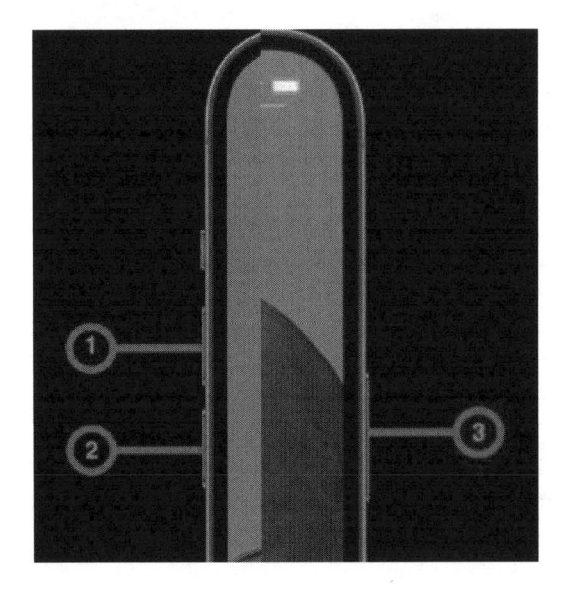

Press and then let go of the Volume Down button quickly.
Release the Side button after holding it down while waiting for the Apple logo to show.
You will see a slider to turn the iPhone off at this point. You should disregard it and keep holding down the Side button until the screen becomes completely dark. The Apple logo will then appear, and the screen will turn back on when the restart is finished.
By using the force restart method, you may avoid completely shutting down the iPhone, which necessitates additional procedures and prolongs the boot-up time.
By navigating to the General section of the Settings app, scrolling to the bottom, and selecting the Shut Down option, you can shut down your iPhone if you so want.

How to Hide the Silent Mode Bell Icon in the Status Bar
The Mute/Silent mode of both iPhone 15 Pro versions is indicated by a crossed-out bell icon next to the time in the status bar, and it will remain in place until you long hold the Action button once again to unmute your smartphone.

This status bar icon may become irritating and inconvenient if you frequently use your iPhone in silent mode, but thankfully Apple has thought to offer a means to remove it. And follow to the directions below.
Launch the Settings app.
Haptics and Tap Sounds.

Turn off the switch next to Show in Status Bar under "Silent Mode."
All there is to it is that. Even with silence mode set, the silence indicator won't show up in the status bar anymore.

How to Transfer Data Over USB-C at 10Gbps Speed on iPhone 15
Instead of using Lightning, Apple's iPhone 15 models all include USB-C ports; however, not every model in the lineup has the same port data transfer speed.
As with the original Lighting port, the USB-C port on the 6.1-inch iPhone 15 and the 6.7-inch iPhone 15 Plus is only capable of USB 2 charging speeds. However, if you're using the appropriate connection and the USB-C connector, the iPhone 15 Pro models allow faster USB 3.2 Gen 2 transfer rates of up to 10Gb/s.

A higher-spec USB-C cable is required for quicker speeds because the USB-C cable that comes with iPhone 15 Pro models only supports USB 2 speeds. Notably, only ProRes files recorded in 4K at 60p may be immediately recorded to an externally connected SSD, even though the iPhone 15 Pro and Pro Max enable USB 3 transfer rates from the new USB-C interface. The iPhone must first be saved to, then subsequently moved from, all other video and picture modes.

How to Adjust Camera Focal Length on iPhone 15 Pro
Users of Apple's iPhone 15 Pro devices may now choose between three different focus lengths when taking pictures with the Main camera.

Apple has added three well-liked focal length settings for the main camera's optical zoom in order to make the most of the upgraded camera system on the iPhone 15 Pro and iPhone 15 Pro Max. There are three standard focal lengths: 24 mm (one optical zoom), 28 mm (two optical zooms), and 35 mm (three optical zooms).

By employing computer processing to trim the 48-megapixel image that the new bigger sensor can record, Apple has made these specific focal lengths accessible to photography aficionados. The results always give a high-resolution 24MP image. By changing the optical zoom setting, you may manually change between different shot lengths. The procedures can be seen in the stages below.

Open the Camera app.
To convert to the 28mm focal length (1.2x optical zoom), tap the circular 1x icon once above the shutter.
To convert back to the 35mm focal length (1.5x optical zoom), tap the circular 1x icon once again.
Tap once again to switch back to the standard 1x focal length.

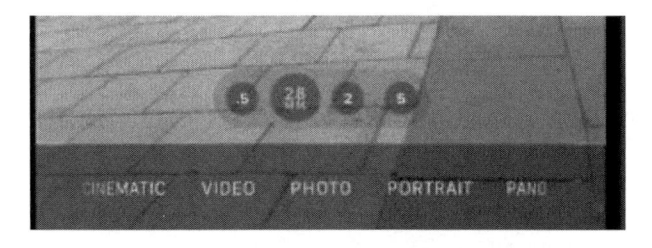

All there is to it is that. Keep in mind that the Camera will provide a zoom ring in place of these focal length options when taking video due to technological limitations.

How to Change Default Focal Length

The ability to alter the default optical zoom setting has been added by Apple, which is helpful if you're dealing with a certain focal length. The procedures are demonstrated in the stages below.
Launch the Settings app.
Tap Camera after swiping down.
Select Main Camera.
Choose from Default to 24mm - 1x, Default to 28mm - 1.2, and Default to 35mm - 1.5x under "Default Lens."

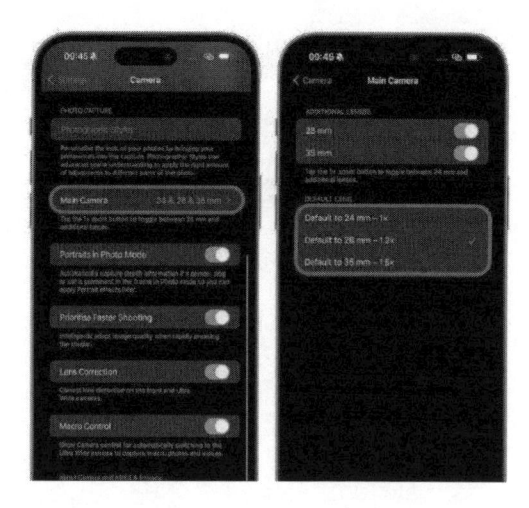

HOW TO DISABLE FOCAL LENGTH PRESETS

You may stop this feature in the Camera app if you find it superfluous or annoying by following these instructions.
Launch the Settings app.
Tap Camera after swiping down.
Select Main Camera.
Toggle the 28mm and/or 35mm lenses' respective switches off under "Additional Lenses."

All you have to do is that. The 1x button will now always result in a 1x optical zoom.

CHAPTER 4: THE LATEST iOS 17 VERSION

On September 18, Apple launched iOS 17, not long after the tech giant conducted its "Wonderlust" event and unveiled the new iPhone 15 series, Apple Watch Series 9 and Apple Watch Ultra 2.

iPhones get a variety of enhancements and additions in iOS 17. It introduces a personalised look for each caller on your phone, with the caller having the option to change their appearance. An iPhone can now be used as a small home hub by placing it horizontally and using the new StandBy function, which also allows Live Activities to be shown in full screen. This information includes the calendar, clock, home controls, and more.

You ought to be able to download the iOS 17 developer beta if you have an iPhone XS or a later model. The complete list of iPhones that are compatible with Apple's latest software update is provided below. And here are some more recent iPhone models to think about buying if your current phone isn't on the list.

Make sure your iPhone is completely updated.
Make sure you have the most recent iOS 16 update before updating to iOS 17 to avoid any problems if you decide to go back. Additionally, it's always a good idea to upgrade your mobile software to the most recent version in case an earlier iOS version has serious bugs or other problems.

Check for any available updates under Settings > General > Software Update to update your iPhone to the most recent version, iOS 16.

To install iOS 17 on your iPhone, first make a backup.

This is crucial: As experimental software, iOS 17 beta may have bugs and flaws that might seriously harm your iPhone. With betas, you never know what to anticipate, so it's important to be ready in advance so that, if you experience serious troubles, you can go back to iOS 16. Your phone can abruptly shutdown or get extremely hot.

Backing up your iPhone while it is still running iOS 16 is the easiest method to accomplish that. The rationale behind this is so that, in the event that you update to iOS 17 and later decide to revert to iOS 16, you will have a recent backup to fall back on in order to preserve your most recent images, text messages, app data, and other data. Your PC and iCloud are now the two options for backing up your iPhone.

Use iCloud to backup your iPhone.
As long as your iPhone is secured, connected to both a power supply and Wi-Fi, and doing a daily backup by default, your phone should work as intended.

Go to Settings > [your name] > iCloud Backup and confirm that Back Up This iPhone is turned on to see if this option is activated. Additionally, you may set Back Up Over Cellular on a 5G iPhone, including the iPhone 12, iPhone 13, and iPhone 14 models, to have your iPhone back up over your cellular network while you aren't connected to W-Fi.

Additionally, you may use iCloud to manually backup your iPhone. Simply hit Back Up Now on the same iCloud Backup screen. You may see the most recent time a successful backup was made beneath that. You may view additional details about your backups, such as backup size, and change what is backed up, under All Device Backups.

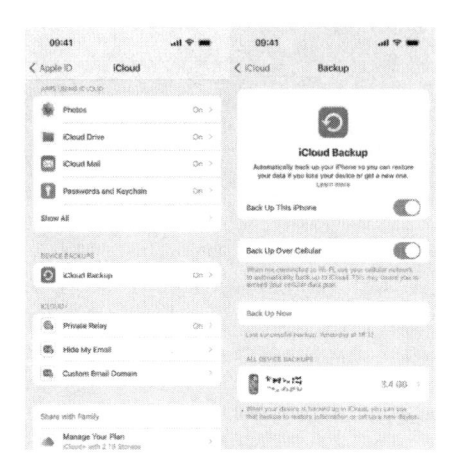

HOW TO DOWNLOAD AND INSTALL iOS 17

You'll be prepared to download and install iOS 17 once you've finished all of the preparations. Go to Settings > General > Software Update on your open iPhone. Hit Install Now for iOS 17 (or Install Tonight if you want to install iOS 17 later) after waiting a few seconds (or minutes) for the update to arrive.

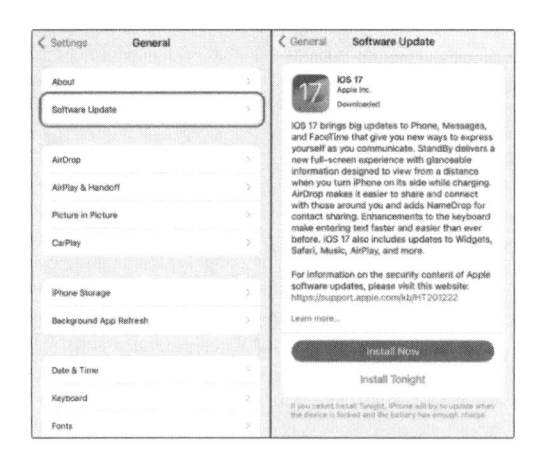

The Upgrade to iOS 17 button is located at the bottom of the page. After clicking it, select Download and Install for iOS 17 if you see the option to download and install iOS 16.6 instead. In order to start the update procedure, enter your passcode.

Once the update process has started, you should see a loading bar and an estimation of how long the download will take. Restart your iPhone when the download is finished and wait for iOS 17 to install. The download of iOS 17 should begin as soon as your iPhone starts up. Just follow any instructions that may appear.

Lock Screen in iOS 17

With StandBy, a feature that transforms an iPhone into a home hub when it's charging and held horizontally, Apple added more improvements to the Lock Screen in iOS 17. Interactive widgets and other features are also included in the upgrade.

How to Use StandBy Mode

In iOS 17, the StandBy mode is on by default. But make sure the toggles are set on by going to Settings ->StandBy.

This iPhone function may be turned on or off using the first toggle, StandBy. It is always turned on.

When turned on, the Always On toggle uses machine learning to turn off the iPhone's display when it is not in use.

The Night Mode area, which you may access when the room illumination is dim, allows you to deploy a crimson version of the UI. By doing this, Standby will prevent nighttime blindness.

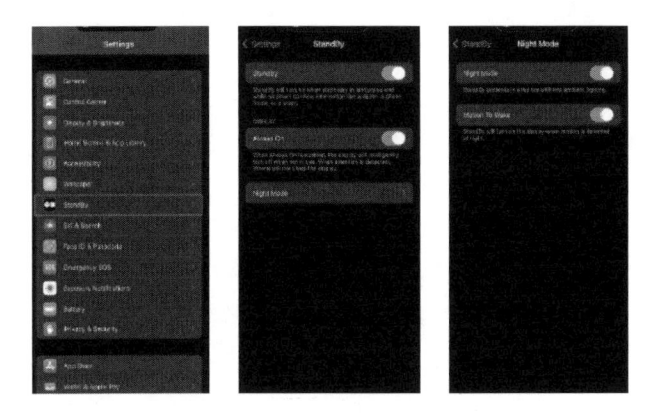

Placing your iPhone horizontally on a wireless or MagSafe charger is the next step. Additionally, you may set your iPhone in Landscape mode while charging it with a cable charger. Make sure the display on your iPhone is locked.

Your iPhone will then immediately turn on iOS 17 StandBy mode. When you use this fantastic function for the very first time, you will get a welcome screen.

You will initially see the default StandBy mode, which shows an analog clock and a calendar widget with the time and date now displayed. The choices offered allow you to alter this perspective.

How to Customize StandBy Mode in iOS 17
On the iPhone, you may personalize StandBy mode by adding different widgets, images, and clock styles. Siri, incoming calls, live activities, bigger alerts, and other features are also supported in StandBy mode. Here are the many settings for StandBy in iOS 17 for the iPhone.

Add widgets to StandBy Mode
The analog clock and calendar widget are what you'll see by default when using the StandBy functionality. To switch the perspective, swipe up on either of them. You may select to show stock prices, weather updates, reminders, upcoming events, or manage your HomeKit gadgets when in StandBy mode, for instance.

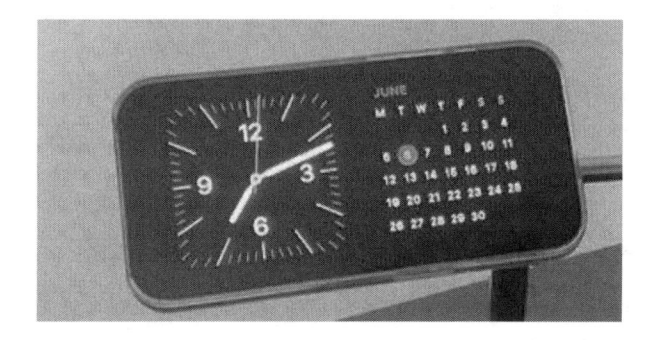

To add or delete StandBy widgets, press and hold either the clock or the calendar.
Tap the '-' symbol in the widget's upper-left corner to delete it.

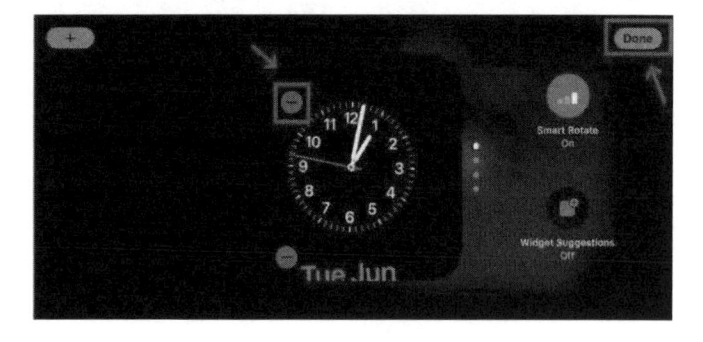

Tap the "+" symbol in the upper left to replace it with a new widget.

Then, select a widget from the list of options in the left pane or use the search box at the top to locate your preferred widget.

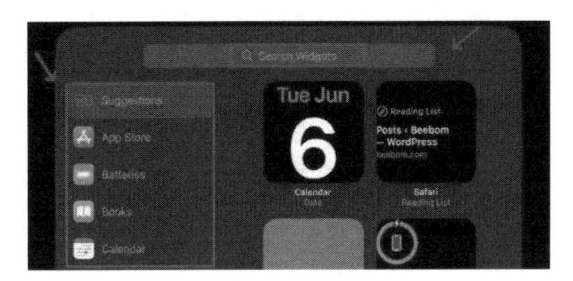

Additionally, you may arrange widgets in stacks that can be accessed in StandBy mode with up and down swipes.
Swipe left on the StandBy view to see all of the accessible displays as you continue.
The Photos StandBy view will appear after the initial left swipe in iOS 17. It shows images and movies from your iPhone's Photos app.

How to Disable Standby Mode on iPhone
On your iPhone, navigate to Settings ->StandBy to turn off this option. The StandBy toggle should now be disabled.

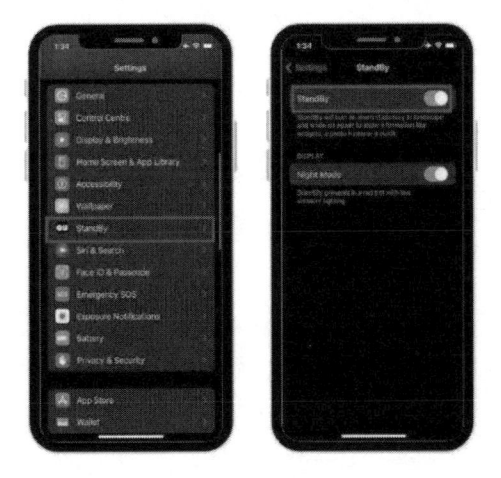

How to Disable Notifications in StandBy Mode
When an iPhone is hooked into a charger and held horizontally (or in landscape orientation), StandBy mode begins to operate. Incoming notifications are displayed in full screen when in StandBy mode. In order to notify you that you have a message, if you receive an iMessage, for instance, the name of the sender and the Messages icon will come up. You can totally block notifications if you wish to keep them from being received in StandBy mode for privacy concerns. The procedures are outlined in the stages below.
- Get your iPhone's Settings app open.

- Press StandBy.
- Turn the switch next to Show Notifications under "Notifications" so that it is grayed out (OFF).

How to Change iPhone Clock Style in StandBy Mode

The time and date are displayed on the third screen of StandBy in a variety of themes that you may swipe through vertically. Some themes additionally display extra data, such as the current temperature or your next alarm. You may change between numerous themes, including Digital, Analogue, World, Solar, and Float, by pressing and holding on any clock.

Three separate clock apps are available: Float, Solar, and World. Float displays the time as large bubble numbers in a variety of color options. Solar features a solar flare design in various hues. The strong numerals in the Digital theme come in a variety of hues, while the accent colors for the Analog theme may be customized. The procedures to follow in order to change the color of the analog and digital clocks are listed below.

On the clock face, press and hold.

In the clock's lower-right corner, press the white button.

From the list of available shades of color that displays, select a different color.

When you're satisfied with your choice, click the X in the top-right corner of the color swatch menu window, and then click Done.

How to Customize the Photos Screen in StandBy Mode
The second screen of StandBy displays material from your photo library with the time overlayed in the upper right corner. In order to prevent unauthorized viewing of your pictures, the iPhone must be unlocked in order to access the interactive and configurable photos interface.

Following that, tapping the image will disclose the date and location as well as a View in Photos button, which when clicked will transport you to the location of the image in your Photo Library.
To choose between themes like Favorites, Nature, Pets, Cities, and People, swipe up or down. Additionally, you may add more albums and hide any themes that you don't like. The procedures are outlined in the stages below.
Swipe left on the opening StandBy mode screen while your iPhone is unlocked, charging, and held horizontally.

The picture that appears on the screen should be pressed and held.
In addition to tapping the eye icon in the top-left corner of each picture collection to include or omit it from StandBy mode (when excluded, the eye icon will have a line across it and the photo will dim), you may swipe up and down to browse the various themes.
Tap the Add button in the top-left corner of the screen, then tap the album you wish to include, to add it to the collection.

If you're satisfied, press Done. If not, tap the minus sign to the left of the album you just added.

HOW TO DISABLE THE RED TINT IN STANDBY MODE
If the room you're in is dark at night, StandBy mode will dim and the display will take on a red tinge to prevent distraction while you're sleeping. Given that it performs similarly to Nightstand Mode on the Apple Watch, it is known as Night mode.

What if, however, you are awake and would want to view StandBy mode at its default brightness level without the red tint? Thankfully, there is an option that will stop Night mode from turning on. The procedures are outlined in the stages below.
- Open the Settings app on your iPhone while it's not in StandBy mode.
- Click StandBy Mode.
- Turn off Night Mode by flipping the switch next to it so that it is in the gray OFF position.
-

MESSAGES UPDATE IOS 17
The Messages app has had a facelift that makes it less crowded and easier to use, and the stickers feature has also been improved. Emoji may now be used as stickers on an iMessage and can be put anywhere. You can even make your own stickers using your own pictures. By enabling loved ones to follow your solo travels, a new Check In function protects you secure.

HOW TO TURN LIVE PHOTOS INTO ANIMATED STICKERS IN MESSAGES
If you've used an iPhone or iPad for a while, you're probably already acquainted with Live shots, which are shots that record 1.5 seconds of video before and after you take a picture in an effort to give static images a little more life and motion. Subjects from your Live Photos may now be turned into Live Stickers in iOS 17 and used in Messages and other apps. Live Stickers, as the name implies, are essentially looping animated stickers that you can share with your loved ones, friends, and the world at large.

It's quite easy to create Live Stickers. For immediate usage in your discussions, build them using the instructions below in the Messages app. Select a contact to send your message to by tapping on an ongoing discussion in Messages or by tapping the Compose button in the upper right.
To the left of the text input area, press the plus button.

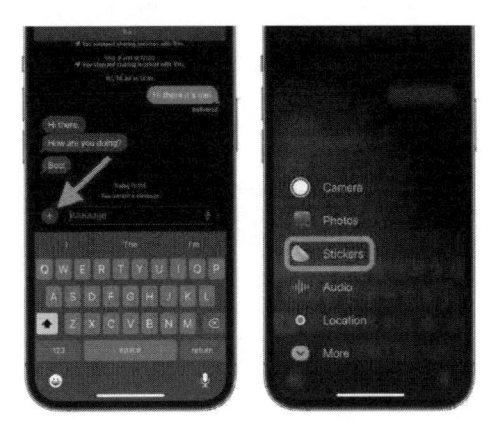

Tap Stickers in the choices column.
The large plus button is located underneath the list of sticker apps.
Next, choose a Live Photo by tapping Live beneath the image search bar.

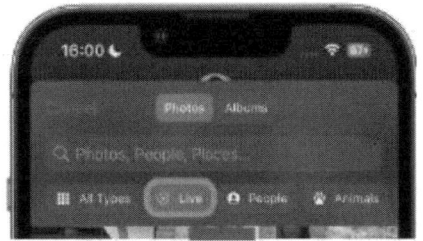

At the bottom of the screen, select Add Sticker.
After selecting the sticker you have created with a press, select Send. As an alternative, hold down the button while dragging the sticker to the beginning of the conversation.

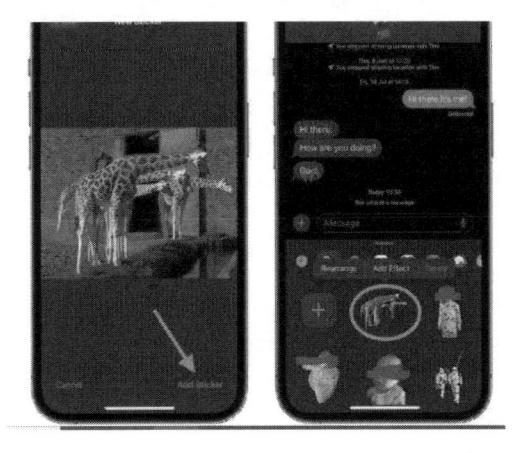

HOW TO CATCH UP IN A MESSAGES CHAT
Keeping up with changes among friends, family, and coworkers can be challenging in a world when practically everyone you know owns a smartphone. This is especially true in group conversations, where

you don't have to put your phone down for very long before you're left behind by the conversation's rapid-fire pace.

For this reason, Apple has added a "Catch Up" option to make it easier for you to stay current. You won't need to manually browse through many messages to pick up where you left off since hitting the button will transport you directly to the place in the discussion that you last read.

When there are messages off-screen that you haven't yet seen, the Catch Up button automatically shows without the need to switch it on in Settings. When necessary, it will appear as a circular button with an upward-pointing chevron in the upper-right corner of the chat window.

HOW TO REORGANIZE YOUR IMESSAGE APPS

The list of applications may be rearranged in the following ways to move your frequently used apps closer to the top, display more apps on the initial menu screen, and more.

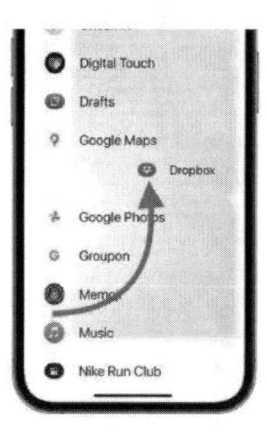

Press and hold an app's icon, drag it to the desired area on the screen, then release your grip. Simply follow the same procedure, but drag the app to the top of the screen and position it where you want to on the first page of icons.

HOW TO DELETE IMESSAGE APPS

You may remove any third-party Messages applications from the list that you no longer require by following these instructions. It should be noted that deleting an iMessage app also removes the associated app from the Home Screen.

- Launch the Settings app.
- Tap Messages after scrolling down.
- Select iMessage Apps.

The Delete button will show when you press the red minus sign next to a program.

How to Auto-Delete Verification Codes in Messages and Mail
Nowadays, a lot of websites and services need users to verify their identities using one-time passcodes that are delivered by SMS or email. However, these codes may quickly fill up your Mail inbox and Messages app.

Thanks to a new setting in iOS 17, those messages may now be set to automatically disappear when the code has been autofilled and used to confirm a login. When you use the autofill function after updating to iOS 17, Apple should ask you whether you want to activate this, but you may toggle it on manually by doing the following.
- On your iPad or iPhone, tap Settings.
- Scroll down and choose Passwords (the following page will ask you to confirm with Face ID).
- Click on Password Options.

Turn on the switch next to Clean Up Automatically under "Verification Codes" so that it is in the green ON position.

How to Send an Audio Message in Apple's Messages App
Before iOS 16, sending voice messages required touching the waveform symbol in the row of applications below the text input area to display a record button. The row of buttons above the keyboard, however, is no longer there in iOS 17, and all that is required to access it is the plus button to the left of the text field.

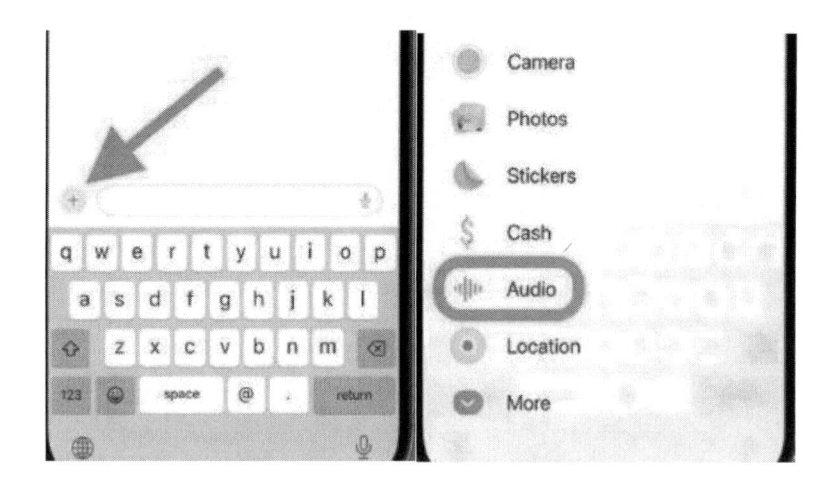

You may discover an Audio button in the vertical list of choices that is displayed when you click the Add button. Since it's simpler to distinguish between options thanks to the bigger icons and text explanations, this design is significantly more straightforward than iOS 16's row of program icons that combined all options.

In iOS 17, all you have to do is hit the Audio button to start recording an audio message. To stop recording, press the red stop button. Then you may send the audio message by tapping the blue arrow, play the recording by hitting the play button, or cancel it by using the X on the left.

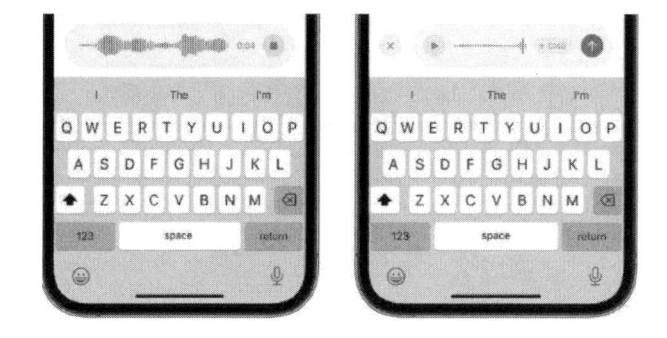

Although Messages' appearance and feel have changed in iOS 17, the interface is actually more configurable today.

How to Add Effects to Stickers in Messages
Users may now make their own stickers from images of things they like, and they can even give individual stickers cute small effects to vary the way they look.

To stylize your stickers, you may apply a variety of effects, such as a white outline, comic-style shading, a puffy 3D appearance, and a dazzling, holographic finish. Your custom stickers will move and reflect light correctly thanks to the sticker effects, giving them a professional appearance.

You can see how to use sticker effects in iOS 17 by following the instructions below.

Tap the Plus button next to the text input area in a Messages chat.

In the vertical list that opens, choose Stickers.

Once a sticker "pops," press and hold it to activate it. Then, select Add Effect from the popup menu.
Choose an effect from the Original, Outline, Comic, Puffy, or Shiny choices by selecting it.
To complete, tap Done.

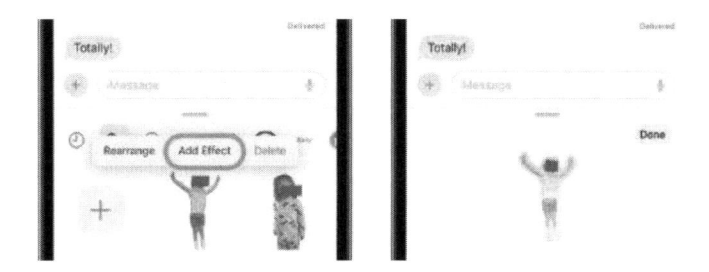

How to turn Emoji into Stickers in Messages
That basically implies you aren't only constrained to bringing them up in discussion anymore. Now you can move them around on a message bubble wherever you like. To make little emoji scenarios, you may even pile them on top of one another.
You may see how it operates on iOS 17 by following these steps.
Tap the Emoji button in the bottom-left corner of the screen while in a Messages chat.
When you have selected an emoji from the list, press and hold it before dragging it up into the message bubble you wish to reply to. Then, let go of your finger.

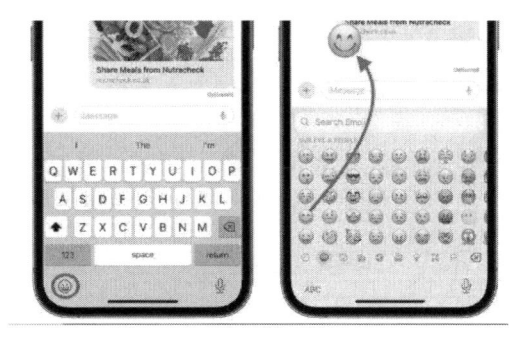

Press and hold the emoji, then select Sticker Details from the popup menu to modify the emoji stickers that are currently displayed in the message bubble.
Swipe left on an emoji sticker, then hit the red Trash icon that appears to erase it.
To resume the conversation, tap Done.

HOW TO SHARE YOUR LOCATION IN THE MESSAGES APP
If you're meeting up with friends or family, you can now share your precise position with them using a new Messages feature in iOS 17. Additionally, you may ask for your friend's location so you can both keep track of one another.
Select Location after tapping the Add button.
Permit Messages to reveal your location: Once or continuously when using the app.
Your current position will be displayed on a map. If you want to share it, click Share and then decide how long you want to share it for: Indefinitely, Until Day's End, or For One Hour. Alternatively, you may hit Request to ask where the person you're speaking to is.
To send the message, tap the blue arrow symbol in the text entry box.

Someone who receives your location will be able to see where you are on a map. For whatever long you decide to disclose your location, they may also find you in the People part of the Find My app.
You must wait for the other person to approve your request for their location. When they do, you'll receive a notification and be able to locate them on the map and in the People part of the Find My app.

HOW TO USE IOS 17 CHECK IN FEATURE IN MESSAGES
You can initiate a Check In conversation with a family member or friend from within Apple's Messages app to let them know when you arrive home safely, whether you're coming home after dark or out for an early-morning run.
As soon as you get there, Check In instantly detects when you're at home and informs your friend. Additionally, you'll be informed when they have been warned and that Check In is complete.

You must pick a discussion with a reliable person, touch the "+" button to the left of the text input box, and then select the Check In option to utilize Check In.

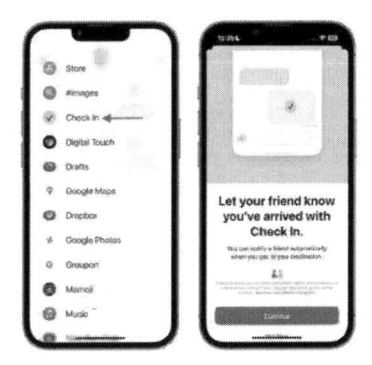

The place you're heading to and the time you plan to arrive may then be entered from there.

The quantity of data you share can be modified. position, network signal, and battery level are shared by Limited and Full, respectively. Full also shares the route taken, the position of the most recent iPhone unlock, and the location of the most recent Apple Watch removal.

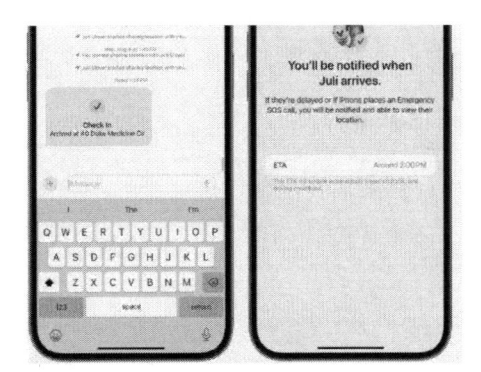

Your friend or family member is informed when you reach your location that you arrived safely and that the Check In process was successful.

PRIVACY AND SECURITY UPDATES

iOS 17 includes a number of privacy and security enhancements, such as limited access to the private browsing tab, the elimination of tracking URLs, safe methods for password sharing, and more.

HOW TO SHARE PASSWORDS WITH FRIENDS AND FAMILY

You may share passwords and passkeys across devices with a group of trusted contacts you create using Family Passwords. (Passkeys enable users to sign into applications and websites using the same methods as those used to unlock their devices: a fingerprint, a facial scan, or a screen lock PIN.)
Passwords and passkeys for shared media accounts, services, invoices, and other accounts may now be distributed to many persons using the new functionality, and each member of the group can access, modify, and add to shared passwords.In iOS 17, follow these steps to create your first Family Passwords group.

- Your iPhone or iPad should now be in the Settings app.
- Tap Passwords after scrolling down.
- Tap Get Started next to the "Family Passwords" card.
- Select Continue.

For your shared group, provide a name, then touch the Add People option to choose dependable contacts.
Tap Create once you're done.
Select the passkeys and passwords you want to add to the brand-new group, then press Move.
Passwords may be accessed at any time on your device by navigating to Settings -> Passwords -> Family Passwords after you've moved them to the group. Additionally, you may manage shared passwords, include or exclude members from the group, and even delete the group if it's no longer wanted.

HOW TO CONTROL WHICH APPS HAVE ACCESS TO YOUR CALENDARS

How to better control how each app may access your calendars with iOS 17. According to Apple, calendar applications with Full Access can view location, invitees, attachments, and notes.

- Launch the Settings app.
- Then choose Privacy & Security.
- Click Calendars.

Tap the application for which you wish to alter access. (Take note that this part also lists the number of calendars and accounts you have open.)

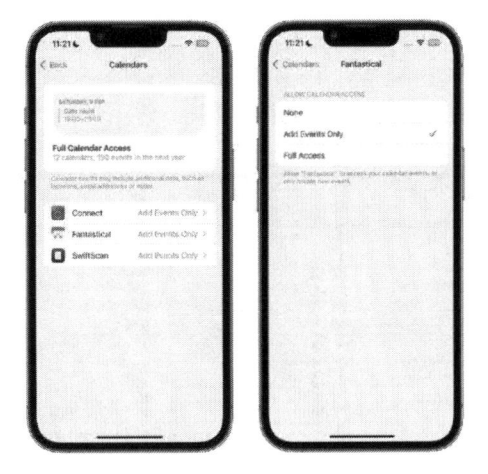

SAFETY
New security features in iOS 17 include offline maps, crucial medication reminders, and sensitive content alerts that stop uninvited nude photographs.

HOW TO MANAGE COMMUNICATION SAFETY FOR YOUR CHILD'S IPHONE
In the screen time settings for your child's account, you can always regulate communication safety. In order to manually enable or disable the functionality on iOS 17-powered devices, follow these procedures.
Launch the Settings app on your iPad or iPhone.
Choosing Screen Time.
Tap the name of a kid in your family group if you are in charge of a child's device.
Tap Communication Safety under "Communication."
Turn on or off the switch next to Communication Safety.

How to Enable Sensitive Content Warnings
It should be noted that this is distinct from the Communication Safety features that Apple has added for kids and is geared for all age groups. The actions listed below can be used to activate sensitive content warnings.

- Open the Settings application.
- Then choose Privacy & Security.
- Select Sensitive Content Warning by scrolling down.
- To activate the option, tap the switch next to Sensitive Content Warning.

You may choose to enable Sensitive Content Warnings for particular services, such as AirDrop, Contacts, Messages, and Video Messages, after the functionality is activated. When the function is activated, it should be noted that Apple's operating system by default blocks all nudity; nevertheless, specific material may always be accessed by tapping on the "Show" button.

SIRI
Saying "Hey Siri" for calling up Siri is no longer necessary in iOS 17; you may just say "Siri." Siri is also capable of reading site content and identifying back-to-back requests.

How to Get Siri to Read Web Articles to You
When you want Siri to read site information aloud for you, there are a few things to bear in mind. In order for it to function, you must first be viewing websites using Apple's Safari browser. Currently, Siri does not react to read requests made in external browsers.

Second, Reader View must be supported by the webpage you want read to you. Nearly all news items on contemporary websites are compatible with Safari's Reader View, which removes graphics, advertisements, and any other supplemental webpage content to leave you with a clear page of readable text.

Look for the words "Reader Available" and the document symbol that momentarily displays in the address bar when a webpage is loaded to determine whether pages support Reader View. The Show Reader option will also be present (i.e., not grayed out) if you tap the aA icon that finally replaces it to denote compatibility.

Holding your iPhone's side button (or iPad's top button) will activate Siri and allow you to ask it to read the selected article to you. After that, say "Read this to me." Simply say, "Siri, read this to me," hands-free, as an alternative.
A media player window will then emerge in the top portion of the screen, allowing you to rewind, fast-forward, modify the volume, and even AirPlay the spoken audio to another device. Siri will then start reading the article to you aloud.

By tapping the Aa symbol in the address bar and selecting the Listen to Page option from the pop-up menu, you can also activate Siri. Siri will start reading the page to you right away.

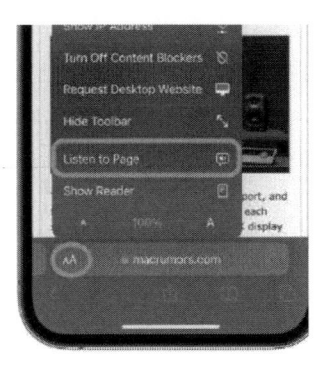

The main difference with this approach is that you won't see a media control box on the screen until you lock your device while Siri is reading. You may stop Siri from reading an article while it is still open in Safari by selecting the Pause Listening option, which has taken the place of the "Listen to Page" option in the Aa pop-up menu.

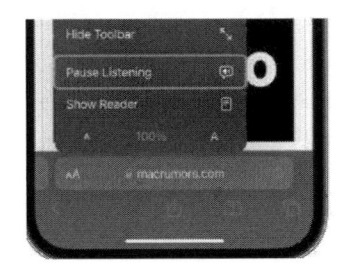

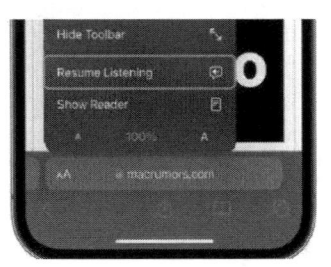

How to Choose Which App Siri Uses to Send a Message
In iOS 17, you can now touch to choose which iPhone app you wish to send a message from when you ask Siri to do so. This enables you to send messages from third-party applications like Telegram and WhatsApp in addition to Apple's built-in Messages app.
Any third-party app whose settings include the "Use with Ask Siri" option is compatible with the functionality. These procedures may be used to see if an app offers the option or to turn it on or off.

- Get your iPhone's Settings app open.
- Toggle Siri & Search on.
- Select the desired app from the list of apps by scrolling down.
- Toggle the Use with Ask Siri option.

How to Force Siri to Listen for 'Hey Siri' Instead of Just 'Siri'

In place of saying "Hey Siri," you may just say "Siri" to activate the voice assistant on your smartphone. Additionally, you may now issue a series of instructions and questions without saying "Siri" again. You don't need to do anything to abbreviate the voice command because "Siri" and "Hey Siri" are both recognized by default by the voice assistant on devices running the most recent version of Apple's mobile operating system.

However, you may restrict your device to just listen for the complete "Hey Siri" command by following the instructions below if the word "Siri" is mistakenly activating Siri in your experience while the whole phrase does not.

- On your iPad or iPhone, tap Settings.
- Toggle Siri & Search on.
- Tap Listen for next to "Ask Siri."
- Choose Hey Siri.

SAFARI

Additionally, there is now a restricted private browsing window that you can't access without Face ID or Touch ID identification. Safari supports profiles for segregating professional and personal browsing (or any other form of surfing you choose to split).

How to Create a Safari Profile

- Simply follow these steps to set up profiles on iPhones running iOS 17:
- Your iPhone or iPad should now be in the Settings app.

- For Safari, scroll below.
- Tap New Profile under the "Profiles" section.

- Choose a profile icon, a name, and a background color.
- Select the preferences for Favorites and New Tabs.
- Click Done.

Your device will set up a "Personal" profile when you create a new profile to distinguish it from prior browsing sessions carried out while using a different profile.

How to Switch Between Profiles in Safari

- Tap the Tabs icon in Safari, which has two overlapping squares.
- To access the menu for the active profile, tap the center icon.

- To switch which profile is active, tap the Profile option.

How to Save Long-Form Web Articles and Other Scrollable Content to Photos on safari

With the addition of the "Save to Photos" option to the Full Page screenshot interface in iOS 17, Apple has expanded the capability so that you can now capture scrollable material in one continuous, vertically scrolling image as well.

The "Save to Photos" option won't show up if the scrollable information is too long, but for the most part, long-form online articles and notes shouldn't be an issue. Also keep in mind that only Apple's own stock apps, including Safari, Notes, and Maps, offer the option to store text as a scrollable picture. You may utilize it by following the steps that are provided, using Safari as an example.

Open the Safari application on your iPad or iPhone.
Go to the website you want to save into a scrollable picture file by clicking on it.
To take a screenshot, simultaneously press the Home and Sleep/Wake buttons. Press the power button and the volume up button simultaneously if your device doesn't have a Home button, such as a 2018 iPad Pro or later.

In the lower left corner of the screen, a preview of the screenshot will appear. To access the Instant Markup interface, tap it. About five seconds will pass before it vanishes.
In the Markup interface's top right corner, select the Full Page tab.

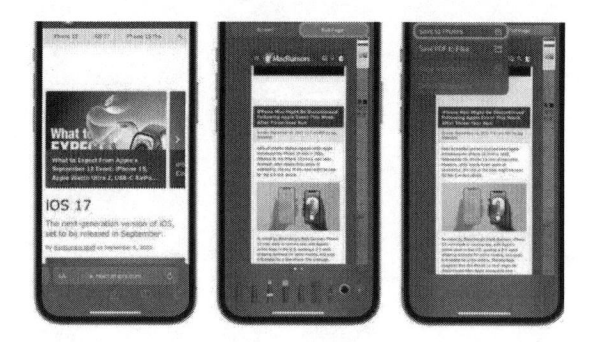

Tap Done, then select Save to Photos to save the scrolling material as a single image. (Be aware that you may modify your photo before saving it to the Photos app by using Markup.)
All there is to it is that. The final image saved in the Photos collection will contain the scrollable information that was taken.

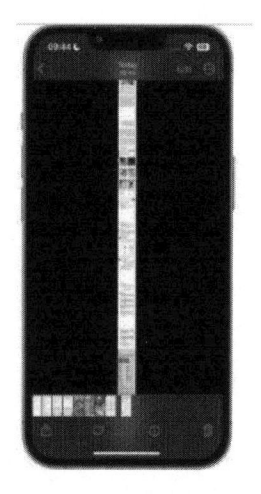

Simply zoom into the material with a double-tap and scroll across it like you would for a typical webpage to read it.

HOW TO REMOVE ALL URL TRACKING IN SAFARI ON IPHONE
- Open your device's Settings application.
- Tap Safari after swiping down.
- Choose Advanced by scrolling all the way down.

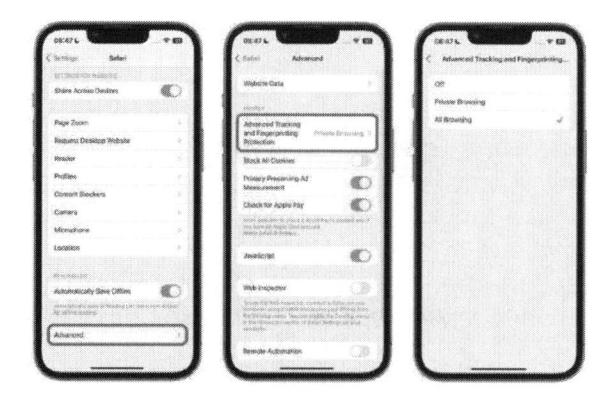

- Tap Advanced Tracking and Fingerprint Protection under "Privacy."
- Click on All Browsing.

How to Disable Private Browsing Authentication in Safari

If you have any Safari Private Browsing tabs open and then quit the app or the session on an iPhone or iPad running iOS 17 or iPadOS 17, Face ID/Touch ID identification or your passcode is now required in order to access those tabs. To put it another way, even if your iPhone or iPad is stolen while unlocked, someone won't be able to access your Private Browsing tabs without your passcode.

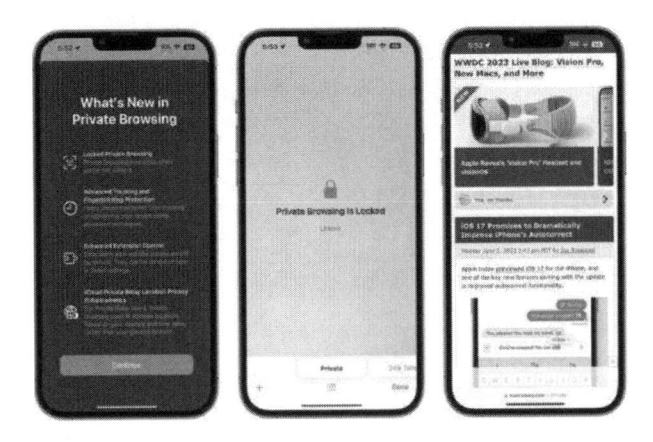

How to Set a Different Default Search Engine When Private Browsing in Safari

With iOS 17, you can now configure various search engines for Safari's regular and Private Browsing modes. For privacy concerns, you might want to use an alternative search engine, such as DuckDuckGo, as your preferred search engine when using standard browsing mode instead of Google.

- Launch the Settings app.
- Tap Safari after swiping down.
- Tap Private Search Engine under "Search" in the menu.

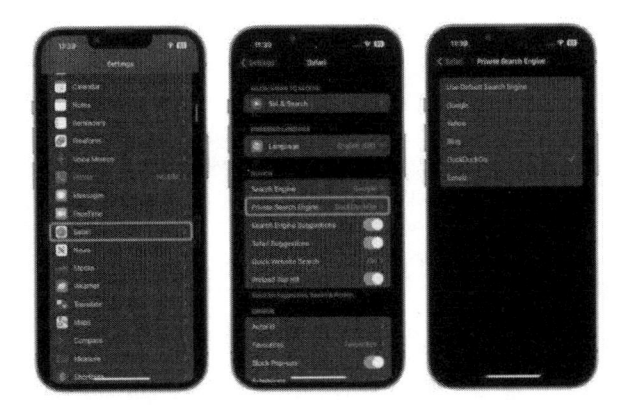

- Select the default search engine of your choice. Use Default Search Engine, Google, Yahoo, Bing, DuckDuckGo, and Ecosia are available options.

How to Clear Safari Web History for a Specific Profile

With iOS 17, Apple allows you to delete your browsing history and website data permanently. Additionally, you may delete the cache for a particular Safari Profile. (Profiles are made to make it easier to divide your browsing into categories like Work, School, or Personal.

- Launch the Settings app.
- Tap Safari after swiping down.
- Click the blue "Clear History and Website Data" button.
- To clear your history, select one of the following options: Last hour, Today, Today and yesterday, or All history.
- Select a single profile from the list or select All Profiles to erase them all.

- Toggle on the switch next to Close All Tabs to close every open tab that is within your timeframe and/or profile(s).
- When asked, select Clear History and then click Yes.

PHONE AND FACETIME

Some of the most noticeable updates to iOS 17 are to the Phone and FaceTime applications. People can see your contact information when you phone them, and you can listen to voicemails while they are being left so you may pick them up if they are important. FaceTime voicemails may also be left because it offers audio and video messages.

HOW TO CREATE YOUR OWN CONTACT POSTER

Personalizable Contact Posters in iOS 17 provide iPhone users a new option to express themselves when making calls.

You may personalize how you're shown when people call you by using Contact Posters. When you call someone, your Contact Poster, which shows on their iPhone, may be customized with images and emoticons. Additionally, you may complement photographs with striking typography, just like the iPhone Lock Screen.

But calls aren't the only place where your Contact Poster appears. Additionally, it is a component of your contact card in the Contacts app, ensuring consistency across all platforms on which you share and converse. Additionally, Apple is providing developers with APIs so that Contact Posters may also be shown in third-party VoIP programs.

As was already said, personalizing your Contact Poster is quite similar to doing the same for your Lock Screen. You may pick the font, color, and picture. On iOS 17-powered devices, the subsequent instructions demonstrate how to accomplish it.

- Tap on your own name in the Contacts app after opening it.
- Select Contact Photo & Poster from the menu.
- Toggle to Edit, then Customize.
- "Tap Poster"

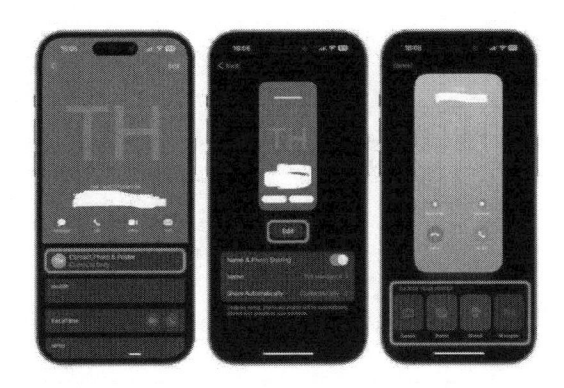

To snap a picture, select a picture from your library, select a Memoji, or make a basic monogram of your initials, utilize the buttons at the bottom of the screen.
The text size, style, and color may all be altered to match the image you've selected. (Note that changing your name requires altering your contact information; it cannot be done via this interface.)
To explore a variety of filters, including black and white, duotone, and color wash in the color of your choosing, swipe over the poster.
When you're ready, press Done to see a sample of what your caller will see. Tap Continue if you like the appearance.

Choosing an alternative photo to use, editing the contact photo's crop, or skipping this step are all options at this point.
Your contact poster and contact photo are now finished. In order to prevent your personalized images from being seen without your consent, Contact Posters may be set up to automatically share with your contacts or to request you to share with everyone who phones you.

How to Record a FaceTime Video or Audio Message
Simply use FaceTime to call someone as usual. You may record a video message using the "Record Video" option that appears after a missed call. When you've finished recording, you'll receive a preview of your video and have the opportunity to try again if it wasn't successful.
Using a missed video call as an example, here's how leaving a FaceTime message on an iOS 17 smartphone works,
- Select a contact from your contacts list to start a video call in FaceTime.
- When they don't respond, choose Record Video.
- After that, hit the Record button to start recording your message and the Stop button to end it.

- To watch the recorded message, press Play. press the Send button if you're satisfied with it; otherwise, press Cancel.
- Once it has been sent, the video message appears in the FaceTime missed call history, where the recipient can view it and give you a call.

HOW TO TRIGGER REACTION EFFECTS IN FACETIME

You may now activate on-screen effects like hearts, balloons, confetti, fireworks, and more when you're on a FaceTime video chat on an iPhone running iOS 17; the effects flood the display above the FaceTime window.

In FaceTime, you may activate these layer screen effects by pressing and holding your image for a long time, which displays a choice of available reactions. Alternatively, you can go hands-free and activate the same reactions by making physical movements. For instance, a Like is initiated by one thumbs up, while Fireworks are accompanied by two thumbs up. A disfavor is indicated by one thumb down, while a rain shower is started by two thumbs down.

New FaceTime Reactions
You can use one of eight reactions during a FaceTime video conversation. They consist of:
- Laser beams
- Love
- Dislike
- Confetti
- Balloons
- Like
- Stormy rain
- Fireworks

Gestures to Trigger Reactions
Here are some physical actions you can take to start the effects:
- Peace sign with two hands - Confetti
- Heart - Heart emoji
- Two thumbs down - Cloud
- Thumbs up - Thumbs up emoji
- Two thumbs up - Fireworks
- Single thumbs down - Thumbs down emoji
- Peace sign with one hand – Balloons
- "Rock on" sign with two hands – Laser

FaceTime already includes these emotions by default, and other applications can add them as well.

Autocorrect and the Keyboard

Apple's autocorrect is now more prudent than ever thanks to a new machine learning algorithm, and it's now simpler to fix any mistakes it makes. Stickers are now located in the same location as emoji so you can use them anywhere in the operating system, and autofill is faster.

How to Use Predictive Autocorrect

Apple claims to have implemented a "transformer language model," which can better tailor autocorrect for specific users, learning your own preferences and word selections to be more helpful while typing. You should notice that the autocorrect recommendations are considerably better at anticipating what you want to say and suggesting words for you to touch to autofill after using iOS 17 for a few weeks.
Autocorrect is less forceful with the automated correction when you use acronyms, shorter words, slang terms, and colloquialisms, but it may still fix inadvertent errors.

Correcting Autocorrect

A blue line will show up beneath the word that autocorrect has changed.

The word you originally wrote will appear (marked by an arrow) when you press the blue line; tap that word to replace it. You will also be given the chance to choose from any other autocorrect alternatives that may be available for what you entered.

AirDrop

By pressing two phones together, the new NameDrop feature of AirDrop allows you to instantly share contact information with someone. There are also additional proximity sharing choices.

How to Send Files and Photos With AirDrop Proximity Sharing

For sharing between Apple devices with iOS 17, this process is still available, but if you're moving between iPhones, you can skip some of the standard sharing stages by using AirDrop's new proximity function.
Select the picture or file you wish to send someone to start the transfer. Then, without having to touch on the sharing Sheet, just place your unlocked iPhone next to the other person's unlocked iPhone, and your device will launch a sharing interface. When you tap the Share button that appears, the photo or file will be sent to the person standing next to you and will be automatically received on their device with permission provided by their proximity.

Enable or Disable AirDrop Proximity Sharing

While the proximity sharing function makes transfers between two devices very painless, we are used to AirDrop operating with someone in the same room and requiring a few manual steps. Of course, you may disable proximity sharing if you don't like the notion. This is how iOS 17 does it.
- Launch the Settings app.
- Go to General ->AirDrop by tapping.

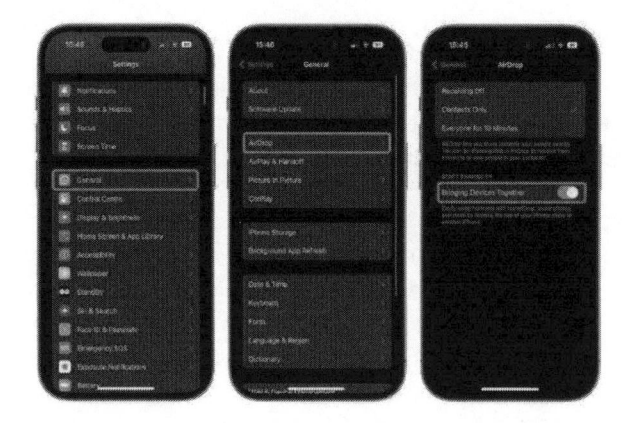

- Turn on or off the switch next to "Bringing Devices Together."

How to Share Contact Details With NameDrop.

NameDrop enables you to just hold your iPhone close to their iPhone to exchange contact information rather than having to put in a new person's phone number to call or text them so that they know your number.

A contact sharing interface will appear immediately when two devices are brought together. When you tap on the popup, contact details and your Contact Poster—a brand-new feature in iOS 17—a image of yourself that you can modify and customize—are displayed. Optional responses on the screen include "Receive Only" and sharing your own contact information.

If the person on the other end is already in your Contacts app, the contact information is updated, and you may pick which phone number and email address to give them. Make sure both your iPhone and the receiver's iPhone have Bluetooth turned on. Utilizing the control center, you may verify and enable the same. From your screen's upper right corner, swipe downward.

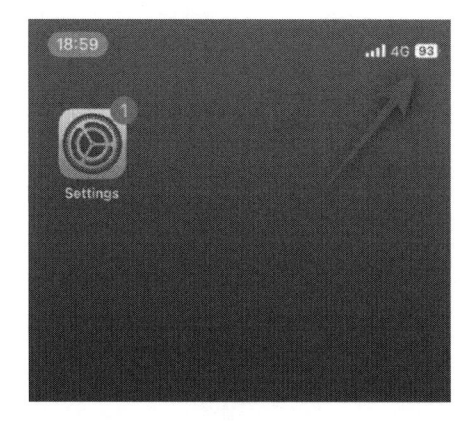

Now activate Bluetooth by tapping the corresponding icon in the connections module.

NameDrop can now be enabled. Tap the Settings app's icon to launch it.

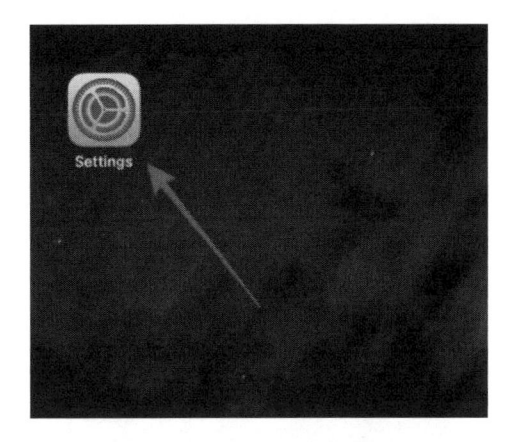

Now tap General.

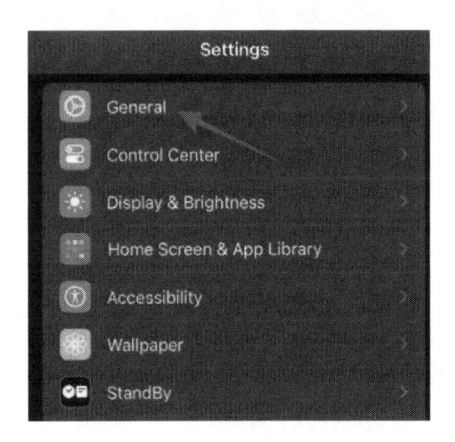

Tap AirDrop.

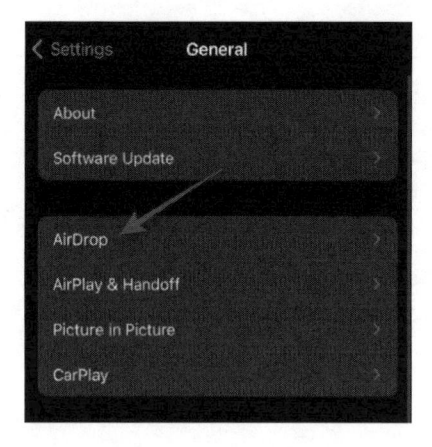

Now touch the Bringing Devices Together toggle under START SHARING BY and turn it on.

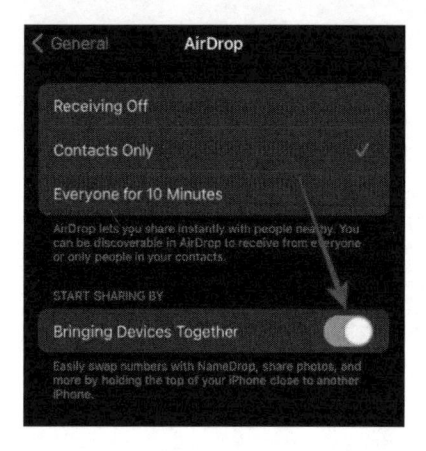

Bring your phone up to the iPhone of the individual with whom you want to share contact information after that. Once the contact information has been transferred, a smooth animation will indicate this. Here is how it appears on both iPhones.
The first thing you will see is your personal contact details. If you simply want the other person's contact information and don't want to provide your own, select Receive simply.
To share a phone number with another person, tap the number that appears next to your name.

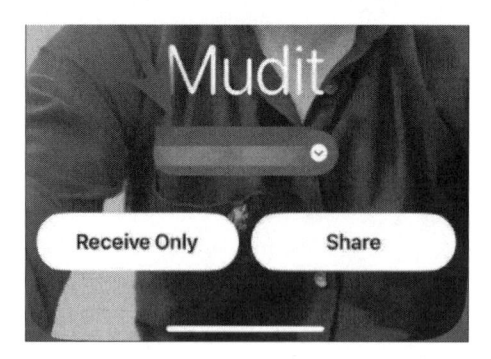

Select the phone number you want to share by tapping it now.
When the other person hits Share, you will be given access to their contact details. Additionally, hit Share instead if you desire to exchange contact information.

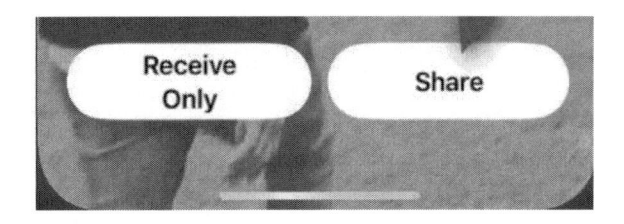

Your contact cards will be shared and appear on your screens as soon as both of you hit Share. To save the contact, tap Done in the top left corner.

And that's how, on an iPhone running iOS 17, you may utilize NameDrop to share contact information with someone.

AIRPLAY
The automatic AirPlay capabilities with TVs and the smarter AirPlay function, which prioritizes the device you AirPlay to most frequently, are two of the new features added to AirPlay.

HOW TO USE AUTOMATIC AIRPLAY WITH SPEAKERS
You may now choose to have your iPhone automatically connect to adjacent speakers while playing content from your favorite AirPlay-compatible apps thanks to a feature that Apple added in iOS 17. You can see how to activate and deactivate the functionality by following these instructions.
- Open your iPhone's Settings app open.
- Press General.
- Select AirPlay& Handoff.

- Tap Autoplay for Media.
- Choose from Automatic, Ask, and Never.

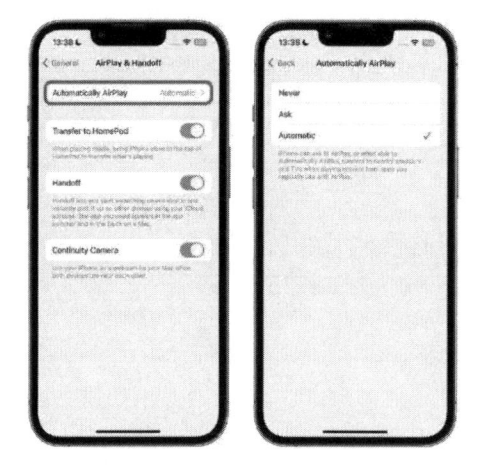

All there is to it is that. Apple is collaborating with hotel chains and TV makers to create smart TV sets that can automatically AirPlay material from hotel guests' Apple devices to the hotel TV as part of another new AirPlay function.

WEATHER

Apple has updated the Weather app to include a new widget for observing moon phases as well as a choice to include the weather from yesterday in the 10-day forecast.

Previous Day's Weather
The opportunity to view yesterday's weather in the 10-day forecast is the largest enhancement. While iOS 16 only allows you to check the current day and the next 10 days, iOS 17 allows you to view the current day, the next 10 days, as well as yesterday's weather.

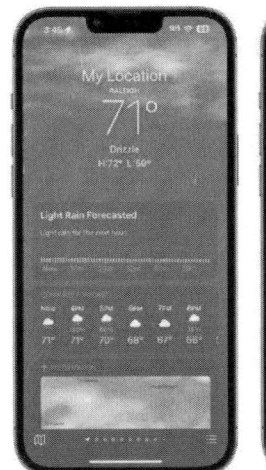

10-day forecasts provide a "daily summary" rather than a prediction and display the likelihood of rain for each day.

Interface Tweaks
A huge "My Location" text box for the weather prediction in your present location has been added to the main Weather interface, along with the city. When navigating between numerous stored cities on iOS 16, it was unclear when it just said the city.

Module Changes
Some of the weather modules have been moved, and the hourly forecasts and rain are now displayed first. The app's news and notifications are shown further down, and a new "Averages" weather module shows how the current temperature differs from the daily historical average. The wind speed module has also been expanded by Apple to include information on gust speed, a daily comparison, and a wind scale.

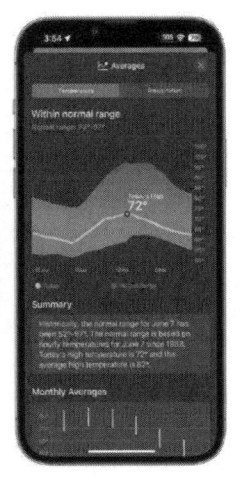

Moon Module
Apple has introduced a moon module that displays the moon's current phase, how long till the next full moon, the periods of moonset and moonrise, and a lunar calendar.

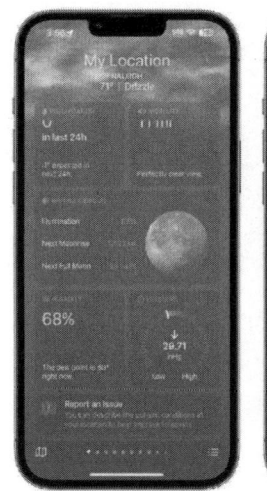

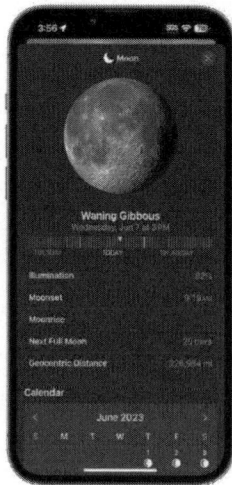

Daily Comparisons
There are options to adjust the units for wind speed, precipitation, pressure, and distance. Daily comparisons are provided for the UV index, humidity, the "Feels Like" index, and visibility.

Data Updates
Despite concerns about the Weather app's accuracy with the addition of the Dark Sky app, Apple does not seem to have made any modifications to the data that is utilized for it.

HOW TO SWITCH MEASUREMENT UNITS IN THE WEATHER APP
You may now alter the unit measures for wind speed, precipitation, pressure, and distance in addition to seeing temperature in Celsius and Fahrenheit.
On an iPhone running iOS 17, the instructions listed below demonstrate how to achieve it.
Tap the three-lined symbol in the bottom-right corner of the screen to go to the Weather forecast display.
Tap the triangular symbol with three dots in the top-right corner of the forecast locations screen.
Using the drop-down option, choose Units.

Use the choices to select your preferred unit for Wind, Precipitation, Pressure, and Distance under the "Other Units" column.

HEALTH
The main new feature in the Health app is mood monitoring, which is intended to help you keep track of your emotions throughout the day and over time, identify what impacts how you feel, and assess the impact of activities like exercise on mood.

How to Track Your Mood With Health app

You may record your mood at various points during the day and enter an overall mood for the day using the Apple Watch or notifications from the Health app.

When you log a mood, a slider bar with possibilities from Very Unpleasant to Neutral to Pleasant is displayed. The aim is to move the slider to the choice that most closely matches your current mood. The selections are color-coded (extremely unpleasant is purple, neutral is blue, and very nice is orange).

After that, Apple prompts you with a list of mood-related words and asks you to choose which one best captures the emotion. Amazed, Peaceful, Joyful, and Calm are just a few of the possibilities available under the "Very Pleasant" mood. Anger, sadness, exhaustion, and stress are among the "Very Unpleasant" emotions. Peaceful, indifferent, and content are among the neutral emotions. You are required to choose one of Apple's options; you are not allowed to insert your own adjective. The goal is to merely select the one that comes the closest match out of the few dozen available possibilities.

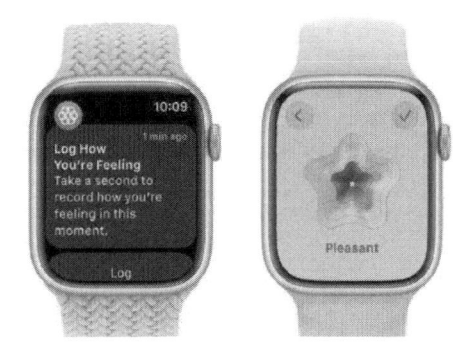

Apple prompts you to choose a mood and an adjective to go with it before requesting the cause of the mood. Health, fitness, family, friends, relationship, dating, the weather, money, and current events are among the options, but once again, you must select from Apple's list. However, you may include context in this section, so you can explain in more detail why you selected a particular category.

- Follow the instructions below to establish your first emotional state or mood journal with iOS 17.
- Choose the Browse tab in the Health app, then hit Mental Wellbeing under "Health Categories."
- Tap State of Mind under "No Data Available."
- Select Get Started.

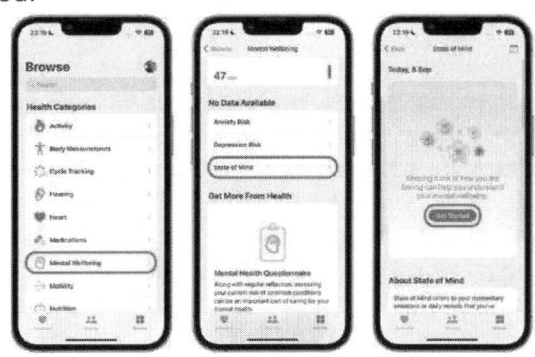

- Select to log Then touch Next to describe how you are feeling right now or how you feel generally today.
- Tap Next after using the slider to record your feelings or mood on a scale from Very Unpleasant to Very Pleasant.
- Select the phrase that most accurately captures this sensation, then touch Next.
- Tap Done after selecting the option that has the most influence on you from the list.

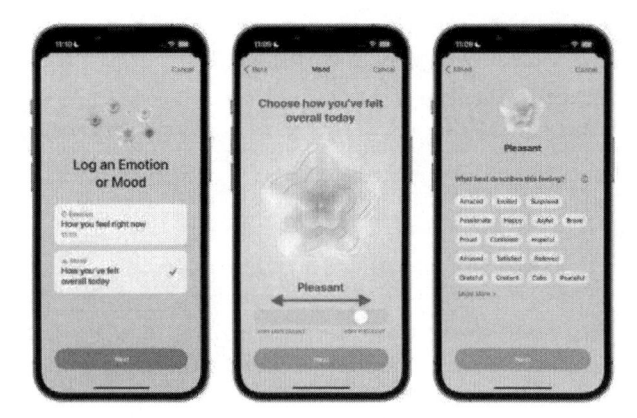

The takeaway is that. Using the State of Mind card in the Mental Wellbeing part of the Health app, you may see all of your records at any moment.

Get Reminders to Log Your State of Mind
You may turn on toggles in the Options menu at the bottom of the State of Mind section to receive reminders to record your emotional state or mood during the day or at the end of the day.

If you want to further customize your reminder, you can choose a certain time each day to receive it using the choose Reminder... option. This feature is helpful if you are aware of when certain triggers tend to happen during your day.

HOW TO GET FOLLOW UP AND CRITICAL MEDICATION REMINDERS
With the addition of Follow Up Reminders for any drugs you track in the Health app, Apple has improved the function in iOS 17. You can choose to get a second reminder if you don't log a medicine within 30 minutes after receiving an official notification in order to ensure that you don't forget to take it.
You may activate Critical Alerts as well as Follow Up Reminders, which display on your iPhone's screen and make a sound even when Focus mode is on or a device is muted.

Here's how to activate Follow Up Medications in iOS 17 if you record your medication intake using the Health app.
- Choose the Browse tab and press Medications in the Health app.
- Optionally, choose the section's bottom by scrolling there.
- Switch on the Follow Up Reminders option.

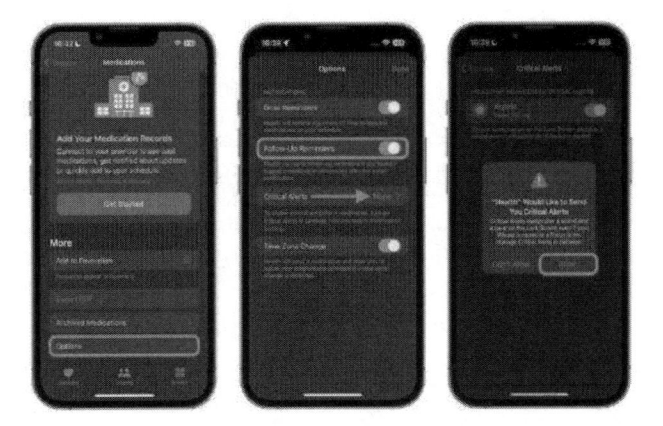

- If you wish to activate them for any or all of your medications, tap Critical Alerts.
- The switches next to the drugs you wish to get crucial alerts for should be turned on. If you're certain, press Allow when prompted.

HOW TO PROTECT YOUR EYES WITH THE SCREEN DISTANCE MEASURING TOOL

Of all, no one is ever too old to take care of their own eyes, which is why adults may utilize the new Screen Distance tools as well. Screen Distance assists you in maintaining the iPhone at the optimal distance to lessen eye strain and the risk of myopia in kids.

Apple will include a posture guide to assist you know where to hold the device for the best viewing experience without straining your eyes, and they advise a viewing distance for the eyes of 12 inches.

Here's how to activate the new function.
- Your iPhone or iPad should now be in the Settings app.
- Select Screen Time.
- Select "Limit Usage," then select "Screen Distance."

- Read the info screen before moving forward.
- Make sure the Screen Distance switch is turned on by moving it to the green position.

Apple's "Shield" will now alert you (or your child) if the iPhone or iPad is too close to the screen and that you need to move it farther away. The shield will show a Continue button so that you may pick up where you left off after the object has been moved to the recommended distance.

Maps

For the first time, Apple has included offline maps to the Maps app, enabling you to download the maps you need for the place you're in or going and use them even when there is no WiFi or cellular service.

How to Download Offline Maps in Apple Maps

You can also access information on place cards like hours and ratings when offline, check your anticipated arrival time, and more. When a linked iPhone is active and within range of the wristwatch, you may even utilize downloaded Apple Maps on the device.

In iOS 17, it's simple to download a map for a specific place in Apple Maps. You may do it by using the instructions below.

In the search box on Maps, type the name of the desired location.
On the information card for the location, tap the Download button.
By centering the frame, select the region of the map you wish to download. Drag the edges and corners to change the size, and the app will indicate how much storage space you'll need to save the file.
Select Download.

The map will be shown in a column with any other maps you have downloaded as it downloads, and you will have the choice to update all of your downloaded maps or download a new map while the map is still downloading. At any moment, you may halt a map download by tapping the progress circle, and you can even delete a map by swiping over it.

When a map is downloaded, Apple Maps will utilize it if you are currently in that area without a data connection. When the last option is disabled, Maps will load real-time data, such as traffic, the next time the internet is accessible, ensuring you get the most recent information.

Limited Service Warnings

The Maps app will suggest that you download the map for offline use if you search for instructions for a route that frequently lacks cellular coverage.

For the time being, this function is only accessible for US National Parks.

Electric Vehicle Charging Stations
Owners of electric vehicles can now see the location of charging stations along their path on Apple Maps in real-time. To only view charging stations that are compatible with their car, users can select a favorite charging station.

Interface Update
Instead of a dropdown menu, the Maps app shows tappable icons for driving, walking, taking public transit, and other options while offering turn-by-turn directions. The dropdown menu that was used in iOS 16 for the arrival time and avoidance settings is still available.

Volume
When you press on the button in the UI for turn-by-turn directions, a new Voice Volume option appears that lets you change how loud the spoken directions are. There are three options: Normal, Louder, and Softer.

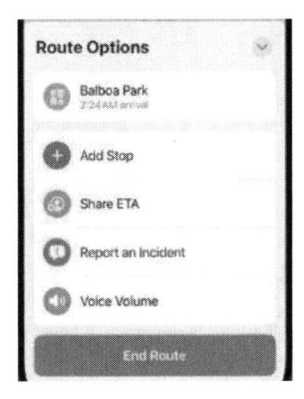

Along with Add Stop, Share ETA, and Report an Incident, there is also a new volume option.

Photos and Camera
Along with recognizing people, the iOS 17 Photos app can detect animals, accurately classifying various cats and dogs. Videos may be utilized with Visual Look Up, and it also works with laundry symbols, recipes, and other things. New leveling tools and an updated QR code interface are available in the Camera app.

How to Name Your Pets in Photos With Pet Recognition
Regular users of Apple's Photos app are probably already aware with the individuals album, which looks for faces in your photos and attempts to identify them so that you may name individuals and use that name as an organizing element in your library or as a discoverable tag.

The Photos app in iOS 17 can distinguish between different animals in addition to people, allowing you to have your pets automatically grouped into albums. As a result, the "People & Pets" record has replaced the "People" album. Cats and dogs may be recognized by the pet feature. Here's how to label the photos of these animals in your photo collection so they are simpler to find and organize.

Open the Photos app on your device.
- Enter "pets" in the search box at the top of the screen after tapping the Search tab.
- Tap any Unnamed Pet under "Pets" (found below the gallery of images tagged as showing pets).
- At the top of the screen, select Add Name.

- After typing the animal's name, select Next.
- To complete, tap Done.

How to Straighten Your Shooting Angle With the New Camera Level Feature
Apple's Camera app has always included a few more settings that may be used to align your photographs. In order to apply the rule of thirds, a Grid may be superimposed over the viewfinder. There is also a somewhat hidden leveling tool for top-down shots that shows a floating crosshair to guide you in aligning your subject.

By removing the camera leveling mechanism from the Grid mode in iOS 17, Apple has improved it even further. Apple has also added an additional horizontal level for more conventional straight-on photographs by making it an individual choice.

When your iPhone detects that you are lined up for a straight-on photo and you tilt your smartphone slightly out of horizontal, turning on the Level option will cause a broken horizontal line to appear on the screen. When your phone is not level, a line appears, which turns yellow after you have successfully oriented it level.

How to Enable the Camera Level
If Grid mode is not active, the new Level option is by default disabled. You may manually turn it on by doing the following.
- Get your iPhone's Settings app open.
- Go down the page and click Camera.
- Turn on the switch next to Level in the "Composition" section.

Try photographing a subject straight on when using the Camera app, and you should notice the broken horizontal lines in the middle of the viewfinder. To join the lines and create a single yellow line, raise your angle straight up. The leveling pop-up doesn't interfere with your purpose to snap an angled shot because it only shows quickly and only at angles that are close to horizontal (in either portrait or landscape mode).

APPLE MUSIC
For a non-stop music experience, Apple has included much-requested features like collaborative playlists and crossfade in iOS 17. New CarPlay sharing features, music credits, and more are included.

How to View Song Credits in Apple Music
An ability to read song credits for each music that is playing, being searched for, or included in a playlist is one of the new features in particular. All of the performing artists, composers, and production and engineering staff are included in the credits. You can easily read the song credits for any tune by doing the following:
- Tap the three-dot symbol next to the relevant music in the Music app on your iPhone or iPad.
- View Credits can be chosen from the pop-up menu.

- To view the credits, scroll below.

You'll observe that the complete lyrics option, which was previously available in the dropdown menu, is now only available on this screen. Additionally, it provides details about the song's audio quality options, such as Lossless or Dolby Atmos.

How to Crossfade Between Songs in Apple Music
The ability to crossfade tracks allows you to seamlessly switch between songs so that the music never stops, which is a new feature that other music streaming services have had for some time. Simply follow these steps to enable crossfade for Apple Music on iPhone and iPad:
- Launch your device's Settings application.
- Tap Music as you go down.
- Toggle the switch next to Crossfade so that it is in the green ON position after scrolling down to the "Audio" section.

You may now select the duration of the crossfade between tracks by adjusting the slider below (it ranges from 1 to 12 seconds).

Try playing an album, customized radio station, or playlist in the Music app now, and you should notice the seamless transition between tracks right away.

NOTES AND REMINDERS

In iOS 17, a number of helpful new features have been added to the Notes and Reminders app. For the first time, you can link one note to another, allowing you to construct documents in the wiki format. In Reminders, there is also new shopping sorting, custom sections, and a column display option.

HOW TO CREATE LINKS BETWEEN APPLE NOTES

In iOS 17, you may easily go from one idea to another by linking notes together with a few clicks. Long pressing on a space in any note is one approach to add a new connection. The second method is to double-tap a word. You have the option of linking only this word or choosing a whole phrase using the highlight anchors.

Then select the newly added "Add Link" option from the pop-up menu. You may use this to connect to a different note by looking up its title or providing a URL. You may add an optional alternate title for the link using the "Name" column, or you can just keep with the original title for simplicity.

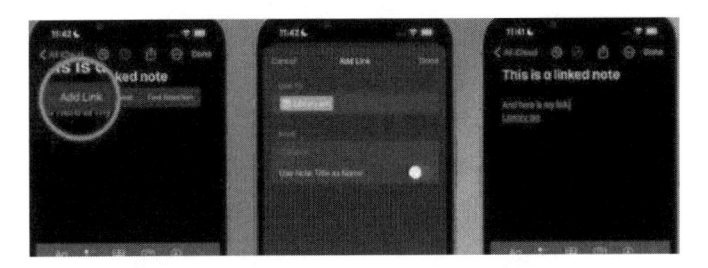

When you're finished, the link will display in your note as highlighted text in the form of a hyperlink, and touching it will take you directly to the note you linked to.
You may add any type of URL with this capability, just like you can with the Edit -> Add Link command in Mac programs. It doesn't simply work for connections between notes.

HOW TO SORT YOUR GROCERIES IN THE REMINDERS APP

When you build a list using the new "Groceries" list type (known as "Shopping" outside of the U.S.), you may include different foods and household items and have them automatically categorized when you create the list. Finding what you need at the grocery store or when shopping is made simpler by the arrangement.

Produce, Breads & Cereals, Frozen Foods, Snacks & Candy, Meat, Dairy, Eggs & Cheese, Bakery, Baking Items, Household Items, Personal Care & Health, and Wine, Beer & Spirits are among the category kinds that are accessible in Reminders.

Here's how to set up an iOS 17 shopping or grocery reminder list.

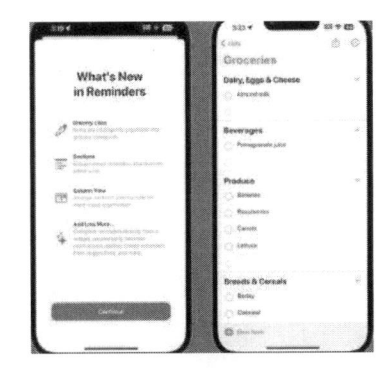

- Tap Add List in the Reminders application.
- Give your list a name, an optional color, and an icon, then touch Done after selecting Groceries (or Shopping) as the "List Type" and giving it a name.

Start adding things to your grocery list. The Reminders app will urge you to move particular things to specific categories as you add new category types. To relocate the object, tap the blue option.
When your list is complete, divide it into several categories to make it simpler to locate comparable goods in the same sections of the shop.

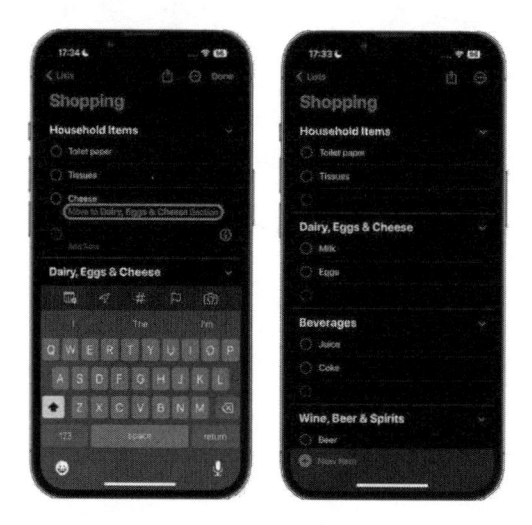

If the iPhone is unable to determine where anything belongs, it is left uncategorized. It is important to take note that it will identify particular brands and types of food, such as "Sour Patch Kids," making it a somewhat robust option for grocery shopping.
The grocery list allows you to add your own categories as well. Simply press the symbol with three circles in it, then choose New Section from the selection. The new section may then be given a name by tapping on it.

OTHER FEATURES
How to Make Haptic Touch Faster on iPhone
Due of the two degrees of pressure that 3D Touch supported, haptic Touch has always operated more slowly than it does. Those who were accustomed to 3D Touch may have considered the Haptic Touch

replacement to be too slow because the first 3D Touch pressure level engaged immediately when pushing on the display.

The good news is that when Haptic Touch is set to the new Fast setting in iOS 17, there is a discernible difference in how quickly haptic options appear when an icon or other on-screen element is long-pressed. Haptic Touch interactions are more similar to 3D Touch interactions because of the speed. On iPhones and iPads running iOS 17 and iPadOS 17, respectively, follow these instructions to activate it.
- Launch the Settings app.
- Click on Accessibility.
- Select "Physical and Motor," then select Touch.
- Haptic Touch, tap.

From Fast, Default, and Slow, pick one. Keep in mind that you may test the speed you choose using the flower image on the same screen. It's still unclear why Apple discontinued 3D Touch. Its lack of discoverability has been compared to the destiny of the Force Touch feature on the Apple Watch, according to some.

HOW TO CHANGE A NEW IPHONE PASSCODE IF YOU FORGET IT
It is now possible to use the old passcode you previously used to reset an iPhone or iPad's new passcode for up to three days after the change is made in iOS 17 and iPadOS 17. In other words, if you're someone who tends to forget a newly formed passcode, Apple allows you to use your old passcode within 72 hours of creating a new one.
After making a change, just touch on the Forgot Passcode? option at the bottom of the screen to utilize the Try Passcode Reset option if you input the wrong passcode on a device running iOS 17. You may use your previous passcode to generate a brand-new passcode by tapping it.

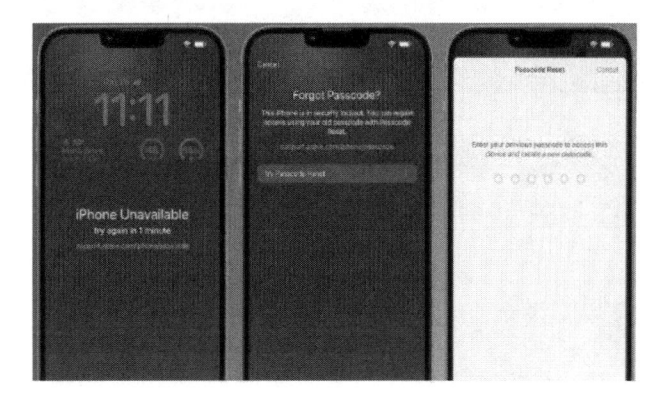

There is also a feature called "Expire Previous Passcode Now" that you may activate to safeguard yourself in case someone has figured out your password. (Note that if you choose this option, you won't

be able to access your smartphone using your old passcode in the event that you forget your new one.) These actions need be followed to use the new option in iOS 17:
- Launch Settings.
- Select Face ID/Touch ID & Passcode by scrolling down.
- Tap Expire Previous Passcode Now under "Temporary Passcode Reset."
- Select Expire Now to make sure.

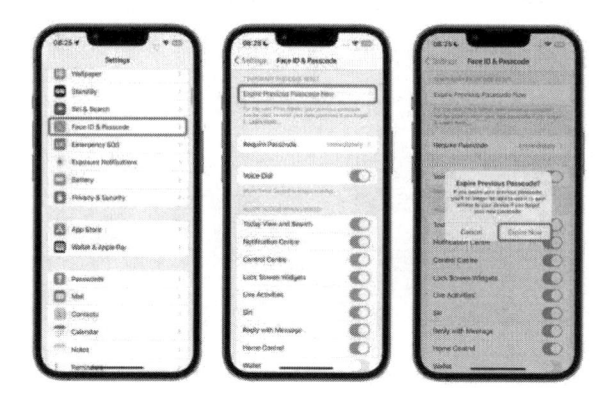

How to Set and Label Multiple Timers

That's accurate. Unbelievably, multiple continuing timers had not previously been possible to establish on iPhones. With iOS 17, the Clock app now makes it possible to set several timers that will count down simultaneously, letting you keep track of many tasks. This feature is useful when cooking a meal that comprises multiple dishes, for example.

You may label timers, which makes it easier for you to distinguish each one in your list of timers, in addition to having many timers ticking down at once. By doing this, you'll always be able to tell which timer is related to which and you'll be able to keep customized timers without having to recall their original purpose.

Swipe down on the Home screen, type "timer," then press the Siri Suggestion to instantly create a timer on your iPhone. Alternatively, you may ask Siri to set a timer with a name by saying "Siri, set a timer called [name] for [duration]." Open the Clock app instead, then select the Timers tab. Choose a period in the timer configuration choices, then touch the Label box and provide a name for it.

If it makes it easier for you to spot the timer, choose a distinctive alert for it. Notably, with iOS 17, you may choose from a number of predefined lengths on the setup page. A timer will be added to your editable list of timers after it is configured. The list will also contain any recently finished timers you utilized as an extra convenience.

The most recent timer you set will show up inside the Dynamic Island on your iPhone if it has one while you are using other features of the device. On the lock screen, the most recent timer will also show up as a Live Activity. You may tap on it to expand it and view any other timers that are active at the same time.

How to Find Your Apple TV Siri Remote Using Your iPhone

Apple secretly updated the software for its second- and third-generation Siri Remotes at the beginning of September. The Apple TV remote control located in the Control Center on an iPhone may be used to locate a misplaced Siri Remote with the updated software, tvOS 17, and iOS 17.

When activated, users will see an interface on their iPhone that resembles Find My and directs them toward the remote. A circle on the screen changes size to direct movement in the appropriate direction. The function is only accessible on the Apple TV 4K versions released in 2021 and 2022, and it is only available on the second and third-generation Siri Remotes.

Additionally, keep in mind that the latest firmware is required and that there is no known way to force the Siri Remote to upgrade. There is no way to force the latest firmware to download; the Apple TV must be up-to-date turned on, and linked to the Siri Remote in order to begin.

Find Your Siri Remote With Your iPhone
Slide down from the top right corner of your iPhone's screen (or slide up from the bottom if your iPhone has a Home button) to open the Control Center.
If it's not already there, manually add the Apple TV Remote button to Control Center by tapping it.
Select the linked Siri Remote on by tapping the chevron next to its name.

Next to the lost Siri Remote, tap the Find button.
To find the remote, use the interface that looks like Find My on the screen. To steer motion in the right direction, the circle's size enlarges. The screen of your iPhone displays a solid white orb when it is directly adjacent to the remote control.

To close the location interface, tap the X button.

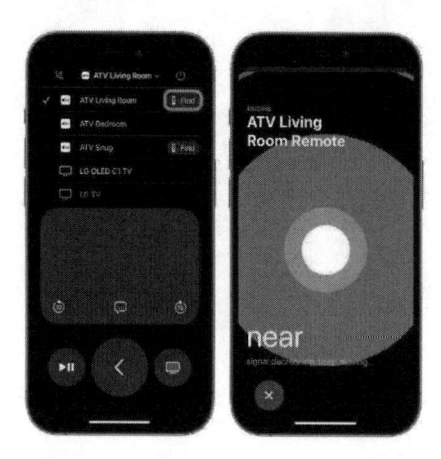

The proximity precision of the tool, in our experience, is comparable to finding an AirTag with Find My, making it really useful for finding your Siri Remote even if it's simply tucked down under the couch cushions.

How to set up Personal Voice on iOS 17

Make sure you're in a quiet area where you'll be alone for around 30 minutes before you begin replicating your voice. You don't require perfect silence, but because you'll be speaking for a while, it's a good idea to talk in a quiet area with little background noise so that your cloned voice sounds natural.

As soon as everything is ready, launch iOS 17 on your iPhone, navigate to Settings > Accessibility > Personal Voice, and then press Create a Personal Voice at the top. Give your voice a name, press the record button, and start reading the phrases that show on the screen after pressing the blue Continue button twice. 150 different, varying-length sentences must be read aloud.

When it says Listening at the bottom of the page, you are free to talk. You don't need to tap anything; just say the phrase, and Personal Voice will automatically move on to the following sentence. You can press the record button to re-record the sentence if you make a mistake. Depending on how rapidly you talk, it should take you 20 to 30 minutes to complete the sentences.

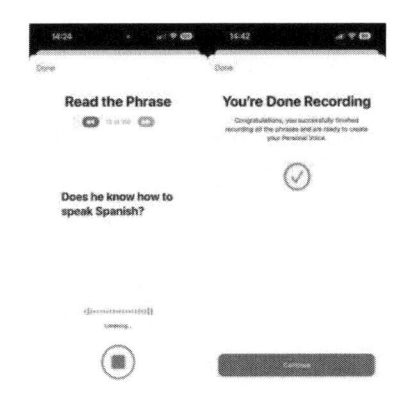

When you're done, click Continue, and the creation of your Personal Voice will start. You must lock your screen and plug your iPhone onto a charger for your Personal Voice to process. When it's ready for usage, you'll get a notification. It took around two days to process My Personal Voice, however processing times might vary based on the individual. Keep in mind that iOS 17 is still in beta, so glitches and problems can make Personal Voice ineffective.

USING PERSONAL VOICE ON IOS 17
You may test out the voice quite easy once you receive the message that your Personal Voice is available for usage. To turn on the Live Speech function, go to Settings > Accessibility > Live Speech and toggle it on. Once enabled, select your Personal Voice, which should be at the top of the Voices section, by going there.

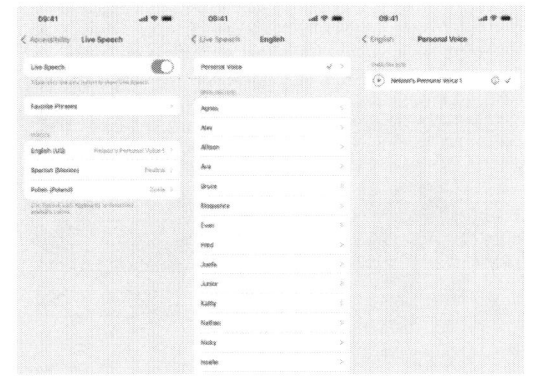

Restart your iPhone or turn on and off Live Speech if you are unable to view your Personal Voice. This ought should resolve any problems.
Simply triple-click your iPhone's side button, choose Live Speech, input the word or phrase you want it to speak in your voice, and then press the Send key on the keyboard. Then, the words you entered will be spoken by your cloned voice. You may utilize this function on FaceTime or during phone calls.

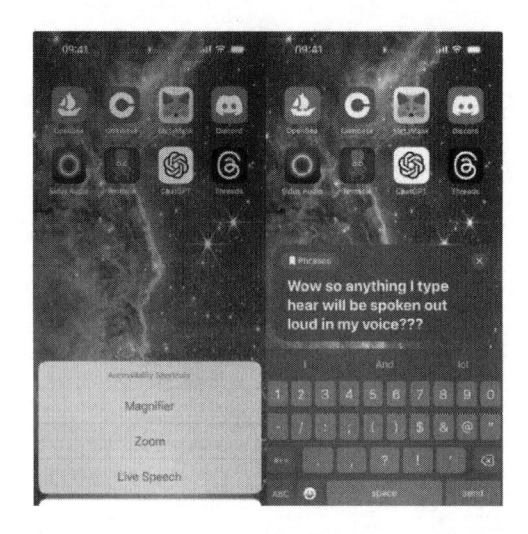

You may add phrases that you wish to appear in the Live Speech feature under Settings > Accessibility > Live Speech > Favorite Phrases so that you don't have to type it out each time. All of your stored phrases will display when you select the Phrases option in Live Speech.

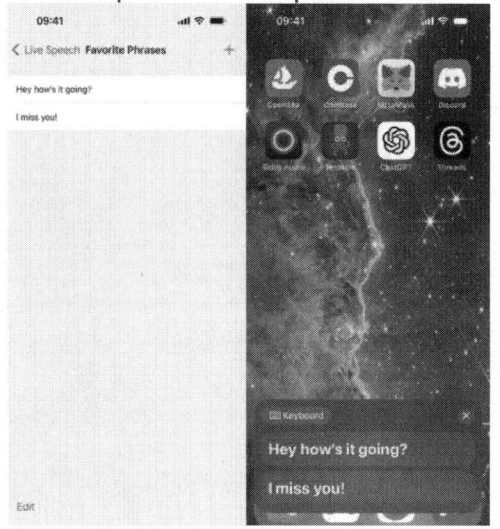

HOW TO SHARE AIRTAGS
- Get the Find My app open.
- At the bottom of your screen, tap Items.
- To share an AirTag with others, tap it.
- Share This AirTag, then choose Add Person.

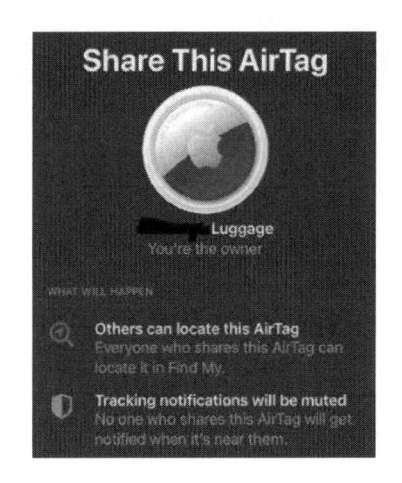

Your iPhone will display a message informing you that after sharing an AirTag, the recipients will be able to find it and won't receive warnings about unidentified tracking. You may then select with whom to distribute the AirTag by tapping Continue.
The other user will get a message to add the AirTag after you've shared it. They only have to touch the Add button on the notice to add the tag to their Find My app. There is an option to press Don't Add if you are going through this procedure and get a notification for a shared AirTag you don't recognize.

HOW TO USE AUDIO MESSAGE TRANSCRIPTIONS
After you downloaded iOS 17, audio message transcriptions were immediately activated. The transcript will show below the audio bars once you send the message. The transcript could be omitted from a lengthy audio message that you hear. If so, a little arrow will appear, which you may press to open a new window with the complete transcript.

Even though your iPhone isn't the newest model, the most recent iOS update adds a lot of useful upgrades. The majority of the improvements feel significant, even if not all of them are huge and showy, like StandBy mode. Several words of advice before the new operating system is released: As a precaution, you should back up your iPhone before updating to iOS 17. Although it may be tempting to download iOS 17 right now, you may want to hold out for a day or two to see if any other people are experiencing issues with their iPhones and to ensure that your device gets the update more quickly.

Chapter 5: Apps and Services

Pre-installed Apps

If you recently purchased an iPhone, you might be wondering why so many applications come pre-installed. After all, there are many of them, and Apple occasionally releases new ones. This chapter is for you if you want to know what all the pre-installed apps on your iPhone are.

App Store

The App Store app, one of the most significant pre-installed apps, enables you to download new programs to your iPhone. You may download any program you want from the program Store, whether you want a free one or wish to pay for a premium one. There are millions of applications accessible for download, so everyone can find something.

Books

Apple has its own e-book and audiobook app called Books. Unlike its rivals, you can pay per book rather than being required to pay a monthly membership fee.

Calendar

You can stay on schedule when traveling with the aid of the Calendar app. You may add your calendar from a different source, such as Google or Outlook, or you can use the built-in Apple calendar software.

Camera

Without the Camera, what would the Photos app be? After all, you will be the one taking the majority of the images in the images folder. The Camera app is crucial for this reason. You can snap pictures with the back camera or selfies with the front-facing camera using the Camera app.

Contacts

The days of having to remember everyone's names and phone numbers are long gone. You may save the names and phone numbers of your friends in the Contacts app so you can contact or text them at any time. To avoid having to input your contacts over when you obtain a new iPhone, you may move them over during setup.

FaceTime

One of the most used iPhone applications is FaceTime. As long as you have an internet connection, FaceTime allows you to video communicate with other iPhone users. Even screen sharing is possible with FaceTime.

Files

Although you might not use the Files app much, it is a crucial program. You may view PDFs and other documents on your iPhone by downloading them using Files from the internet.

Find My

Do you frequently misplace your iPhone or other electronic devices? If so, you could frequently utilize the Find My app. The Find My app may be used to find your MacBook, AirPods, and other gadgets, but you can't use it without a phone. If you misplaced your own iPhone, you may still use this app on a friend's iPhone.

Health

The Apple Health app will track your activities and provide various health information. You can combine your data and keep track of your statistics here if you own an Apple Watch.

iTunes Store
The iTunes store app enables you to get new material for your iPhone similarly to the App Store. It assists you in downloading music, movies, and TV shows but does not download applications. New ringtones may also be downloaded from the iTunes store. The iTunes Store will preserve your previous purchases so you may download them again whenever you want if you've previously made something from there.

Mail
You might want to spend some time configuring the Mail app if you're always on the move. You may access all of your emails and email accounts at once with Mail. On the move, you may read and respond to emails, as well as transmit documents via the Files app.

Maps
You might want to spend some time configuring the Mail app if you're always on the move. You may access all of your emails and email accounts at once with Mail. On the move, you may read and respond to emails, as well as transmit documents via the Files app.

Notes
You can arrange your ideas and keep track of important details with the aid of the useful app notes. You can compose lists, jot down thoughts, and even construct charts with the Notes app. Therefore, you won't lose your thoughts, the Notes app will also back them up to iCloud.

Phone
The app that lets you place and receive calls is called Phone. You may listen to and check your voicemail from this location. The Phone call records also contain information on FaceTime calls. Additionally, you may add your preferred contacts to create a speed dial-like feature.

Photos
Viewing any photo you take is possible in the Photos app. You may also view any screenshots or images you've saved from Safari using this app. You may organize your Photos using the folders in this program.

Safari
The browser application Safari is available on other Apple products, such as MacBooks. You can use this application to browse the internet. Additionally, it will save the websites you visit the most on the home page for quick access. There are alternative browsers available for download in the App Store if you'd rather use one of those to access the internet.

How to Use Other Apps and Services

Use App Clips
On your iPhone, there is an app for pretty much everything you may want to do, but sometimes you don't have the app you require at the time you require it, for example, a specific parking app while paying for parking. App Clips fill this role. An app clip, which can be used to order coffee or rent a scooter, is a little section of the app that is concentrated on a single activity and created to appear when you need it.

The software Store or finding the right software on your iPhone, both of which take far longer than the App Clip launching will, are no longer necessary because App Clips are small (under 10MB) and launch quickly at the bottom of your iPhone. App Clips, as their name implies, are little excerpts or videos of an app that highlight the specific features you require, like the parking payment page.

How do App Clips work?
You can find App Clips through App Clip codes, NFC tags, or QR codes, scanning them with your iPhone's camera, or tapping the NFC tag, if one is available for the app you need right now. They can also be started from the Recents section of the App Library, Maps, Messages, Safari, and that app's menu.

Your iPhone's display will show an App Clip card with the option to "Open" the App Clip at the bottom. Below the app's name and adjacent to the Open action button is a list of the tasks the App Clip will accomplish when you tap on Open.

When you scan the code on the scooter, for instance, a Spin App Clip with the message "Tap Open to unlock this scooter and ride" will show at the bottom of your iPhone.

When you tap open, the option to accept the terms and conditions and use Apple Pay will then be presented. There is an option to access the entire app in the App Store at the top of the page if you wish to download it or view it if you already have it on your iPhone, but you won't need to open the full app to finish the assignment.

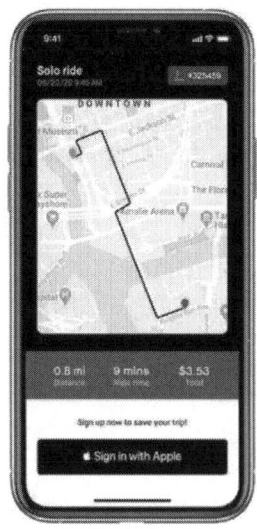

You may sign in by using For those apps that require an account, sign up with Apple, and then use Apple Pay to instantly complete transactions. This makes everything quick, easy, and secure. The App Clip will vanish once you've completed the assignment.

A selection of the apps that offer App Clips are shown below:
- Spin
- Unwind

- Etsy
- Phoenix 2
- Drop Recipes
- Park Whiz
- Panera Bread
- Quit Anger
- ChibiStudio
- Parcel - Delivery Tracking
- SignEasy
- SmartGym
- WaterMinder
- CardPointers

How to Install New Fonts on an iPhone

The iPhone and iPad aren't as flexible when it comes to using custom typefaces as Android, let alone Windows or macOS. Custom fonts can only be installed on Apple mobile devices by looking for fonts apps in the App Store. There are several options, but some require very pricey yearly subscriptions. Fonts and iFont are the two with the best free selections.

Scroll through the Fonts app until you find the desired styles, then press Install on each one. You may access Google Fonts, Dafont, Fontspace, and even install TTF font files from cloud storage using iFont, giving you more options.

You'll be prompted to confirm after selecting Install in the Fonts app. Once you've done so, fresh fonts will show up in Settings > General > Fonts.

iFont functions a little differently. To get it, you must touch Get after choosing one. However, it doesn't add the font to Settings' Fonts area. In its place, Settings > General > VPN and Device Management produces a configuration profile. Since fonts aren't all in one place, this may be pretty frustrating.

HOW TO USE FREEFORM APP
With the help of the software Freeform, you can generate ideas without being constrained by an outliner or list tool. On an iPhone or iPad, you can utilize text, photos, shapes, and lines, create lists and sticky notes, and draw with your finger or an Apple Pencil.

In essence, it serves as a sizable digital whiteboard where several users can annotate and draw at once. You can watch where and what other people are working thanks to individual cursors.
 The benefit of this is that you may make real-time additions to another person's work as they develop an idea or add details, and the other person can reciprocate for your contributions.

So, how do you use Freeform?
On phones and tablets as opposed to desktop, the user interface is set up significantly differently, and there are extras like Apple Pencil compatibility. However, regardless of the platform you use, Apple has made a lot of effort to keep the Freeform experience comparable. We make use of Freeform for Mac in this manual.

Freeform boards
You can view your previously created boards when you launch the Freeform app or create a new one. By allowing them to be sorted by favorites or shared, Apple provides these boards some organization. Your boards are on the left, and in the upper right corner, there is a Share button that you can use to share them.
You can create new boards or modify existing ones using a variety of tools. Along with doodling on the blank digital page, you can also add files and documents including images, PDFs, URLs to websites, audio snippets, and videos.

Sticky notes
One of my most popular tools is the sticky note. These can be positioned anywhere on your board. This is the best way to write notes or remarks to your whiteboard when working alone or with others. There are numerous colors, font sizes, and typefaces available for sticky notes. There are innumerable shapes, from everyday objects to activities. Of course, you also have access to a complete collection of drawing tools.

Freeform easy sharing
The Freeform app's ability to run on all Apple devices is one of its strongest features. As a result, it's excellent for collaboration, which is one of its key benefits. Real-time collaboration is simple because anything you and your coworkers (up to 100 individuals per board) accomplish instantly appears on the canvas. The modifications to a board that you share by FaceTime, email, or a link will be visible in the board's Messages thread. You can modify who has access, whether they can make changes, and if they can invite other people when you click the Share button.

How to use Find My
Do you now fear that your device has been stolen or have you lost it? It's time to locate it. We'll start by showing you how to accomplish it from another iPhone, iPod, or iPad.
If you don't already have it, download the Find My iPhone app first.
Navigate to the Devices page in the app to find your device's location (or, at the very least, the last position it was seen). Additionally, you have the option to wipe the concerned lost gadget or play an alarm from it.

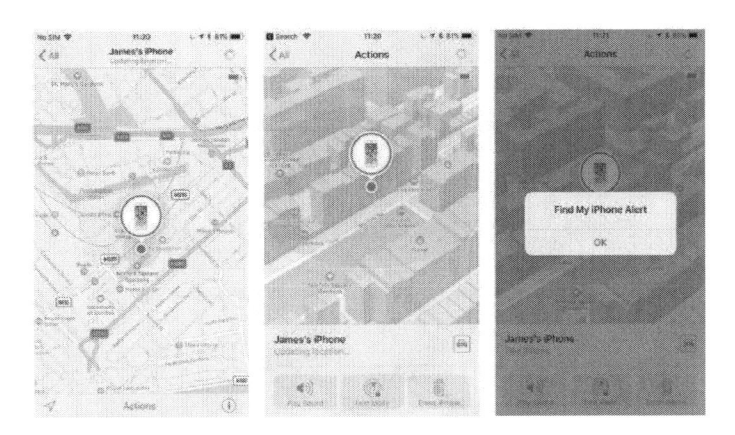

Side note: Anyone with whose iPhone you have authorized to share location information can be found with the Find My Friends app. Although there aren't many tracking options offered by the app, it does offer a quick and simple way to check if your child or significant other has lost their iPhone.

How to Mark an Apple Device as Lost in the Find My App
The first line of defense against losing or having your iPhone or iPad stolen is to use Find My. With the ability to lock your device and efficiently track it, you may render it practically useless to anyone trying to find or steal it. Your iPhone or iPad most likely already has Find My enabled because it does it automatically after you set up your device and log in with your Apple ID.

Activation Lock, which allows you to remotely lock your device by putting it in Lost Mode, is Find My iPhone's most potent feature. By doing this, you'll be able to remotely password-protect the device and add a personalized message on its Lock Screen, enabling someone to contact you and set up a meet-up if they find your lost phone or tablet. It's also important to note that when your device is in Lost Mode, only your Apple ID and password can restore or reactivate it. At the very least, this will stop the potential burglar from doing anything with your smartphone even if it doesn't stop them from stealing it.

Both the Find My app on any iOS device and iCloud.com via a web browser can be used to activate Lost Mode. I'm using my iPhone to search for my missing iPad in the stages that follow. On a stolen iPhone, iPod touch, Apple Watch, or Mac, the procedure for activating Lost Mode is similar.

Open the Apple Find My app that is already loaded on your iPhone, iPad, iPod touch, or Mac. If you don't possess another Apple device, you can utilize iCloud.com in a web browser or the Find My app on an iPhone or iPad belonging to a family member or friend (more on this below). Keep in mind that you must sign in with the same Apple ID and password that you used to set up the device for Lost Mode.
Enter the Find My app and select the Devices tab.

A map and a list of the devices connected to your Apple ID will be displayed by Find My. The lost or stolen device should be tapped. It is my iPad Pro in this instance.

Swipe up to reveal extra options if you're using an iPhone, iPad, or iPod touch. To view more information about a device, click the info button on a Mac.
Under the Mark As Lost heading, select Activate.

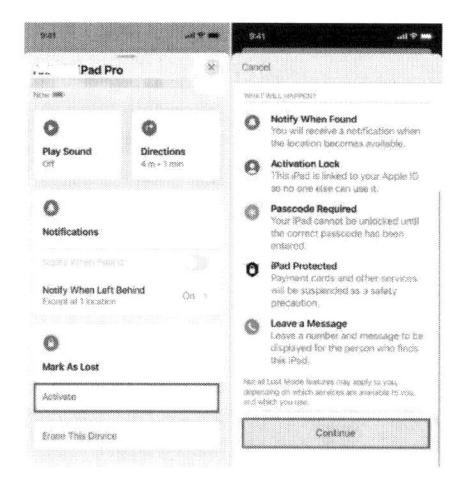

When you mark the device as lost, the following will happen as a summary:
Notify When Found: If and when the location becomes available, you'll be notified.
Activation Lock: No one else can use this gadget because it is connected to your Apple ID.
Passcode Required: The proper passcode must be entered before your device may be unlocked.
Device Protected: Services such as credit cards and others will be suspended out of an abundance of caution.
Leave a Message: For the person who finds this iPad, provide a phone number and a note that will be displayed.
Tap Continue.
Find My will need you to create a passcode right away if the device you're trying to place in Lost Mode doesn't already have one. Enter a passcode, then input it again to confirm the new passcode. You can move on to the next step if the device already has a passcode activated.

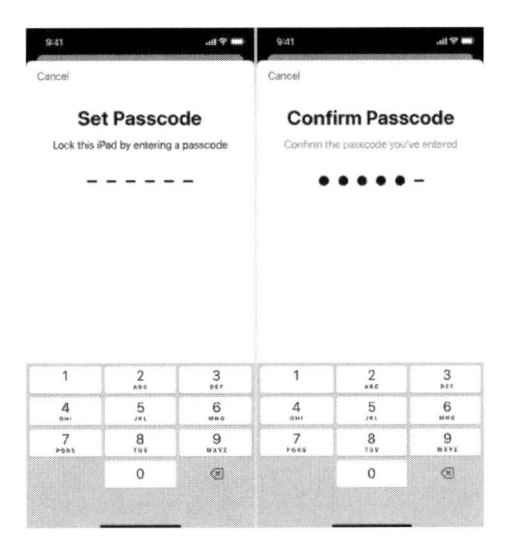

Tap Next after entering a phone number that will appear on the stolen or lost device. Although it is optional, it is strongly advised that you include your phone number so that you may be reached if someone finds your device. It can be a contact number you have on you or that of a friend or family member.

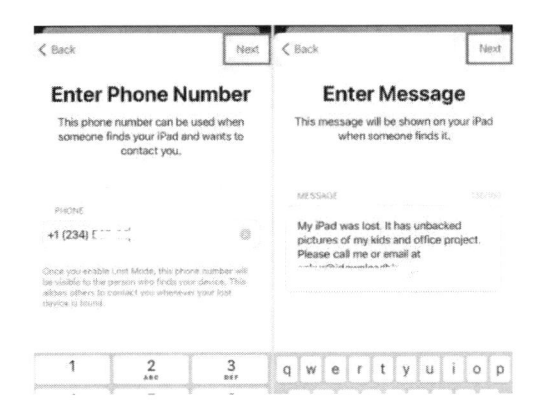

Tap Next after typing a message of up to 160 characters. The message is "This iPhone/iPad has been lost." by default. Please give me a call," but you may alter it whatever you choose. This message will be shown to the finder, just like the phone number will. You may provide your email address or a note requesting that the finder return your device here.

Check the phone number, the message that was inserted, maintain Notify When Found enabled, and then hit Activate. Make sure to stay on this page until the processing is through and it returns you to the Find My app.

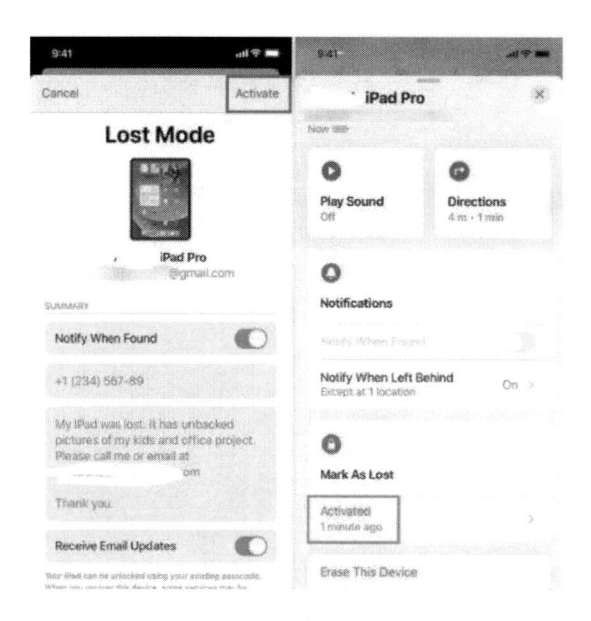

- Save a webpage with annotations as a PDF.
- Describe yourself to Siri.
- Text and document scanning
- Create voicemail
- Verify voicemail
- Modify the voicemail message and settings
- to read a QR code
- Calendar events may be created and edited.
- Control your purchases, subscriptions, preferences, and limitations.
- Employ the stopwatch.
- Block obtrusive callers

Chapter 6: iPad, iWatch, and airpods

iPadOS 17

Every year, Apple releases a big software update for all of its products, including the iPad, Mac, Apple Watch, and the iPhone. iOS 17 for the iPhone and watchOS 10 for the Apple Watch have both been released as software updates. However, iPadOS 17 is what brings about the new features on the iPad. What features are now accessible on iPad, which iPad models are compatible, and how to download and install iPadOS 17 are all covered in this guide to iPadOS 17.

During its Worldwide Developer Conference, popularly known as WWDC, on June 5, Apple unveiled iPadOS 17 along with iOS 17, watchOS 10, macOS Sonoma, and a variety of hardware updates. iPadOS 17's final build has now been made available for download after the public beta version was made available in July 2023. As of September 18, 2023, iPadOS 17 is available for download and installation.

iPadOS 17 features
With iPadOS 17, all of these essential functionalities are now accessible on the device.

Lock Screen
With iPadOS 17, the modifications made to the Lock Screen in iOS 16 are carried over to the tablet. There are several options to customize it, including a variety of wallpapers like Astronomy and Kaleidoscope and Widgets. As well as Live Activities on Lock Screen, which will allow you to keep current with just a fast glimpse, there is a motion effect for Live Photo wallpaper that gives your Live Photos on your Lock Screen a little more life.

Interactive Widgets
iPadOS 17 introduces Interactive Widgets, much like iOS 17. These eliminate the need to launch each individual program by allowing you to do actions straight from the widget on the Home Screen or Lock Screen, such as playing music or turning off the lights.

Health
With iPadOS 17, the Health app is available for the first time on the iPad and has been optimized for the bigger display. The favorites view offers lots of detail, and interactive charts let you evaluate trends and standout information. There is a focus on mental health, and you may schedule medication reminders and report symptoms as well. The mental health elements urge you to consider your emotional condition and examine insightful information about what could be causing it. You can also access standardized tests that clinics use to determine the likelihood of depression or anxiety. Additionally, there are a few functions in the iPad's Health app that are related to eye health.

FaceTime
With iPadOS 17, FaceTime receives a minor upgrade, but there are a few new features. When someone misses your FaceTime call, you can leave them an audio or video message. FaceTime is also compatible with Apple TV. You may also respond by using hand gestures, such as a double thumbs up, which will cause 3D augmented reality effects, such as hearts, confetti, and fireworks, to fill the camera frame.

Messages
With iPadOS 17, Messages gains a number of new features, including the ability to swipe to reply and transcription for audio messages. We are extremely happy to see both of these additions. Additionally, iMessage applications are moving to be all in one place for faster access via a new plus button, and search is being improved with criteria that you can combine to make it easier and quicker for you to discover anything in your conversations. With iPadOS 17 and the plus button, sharing a location through

texts is also simpler. Using the plus button, you may share your location or ask a friend for their location, and the information will be shown right away in the Messages chat with that person.

Stickers
In addition to Animoji, Memoji, and emoji, the new Stickers drawer in iPadOS 17 and iOS 17 allows you to view all of your stickers in one location. Stickers sync with iCloud so that you can access them from any device and use them everywhere emoji are accessible, including in third-party apps. Additionally, Live Stickers may be made and used to reply to messages.

PDFs and Notes
With iPadOS 17, Notes gains a variety of capabilities, some of which are really helpful. With the updated software, you may annotate a PDF right from the Notes app and utilize Enhanced AutoFill to leverage your stored Contacts information to automatically fill out information on a PDF or scanned document. Additionally, you may work together on PDFs and receive real-time updates on any modifications. Last but not least, iPadOS 17 enables you to group together relevant Notes, such as a Christmas shopping list and packing list.

Safari
Making a profile that separates your history, extensions, Tab Groups, cookies, and favorites is one of Safari's new capabilities. It implies that you may have different profiles for different purposes, such as work and personal, and move between them as needed. With iPadOS 17, search is also more responsive. The Autofill verification codes we receive in mail are perhaps our favorite new Safari feature. It will now do this action automatically; you no longer need to launch Mail, copy the verification code, and then return to Safari to input it.

Keyboard
In iPadOS 17, autocorrect receives some love and is more accurate to help users type the correct word the first time. When a word is autocorrected, it is briefly highlighted, and if it is incorrect, you may quickly return to the original word by tapping it. You may also use the space bar to complete phrases or sentences in their entirety.

Freeform
Freeform received a few updates with iPadOS 17, however it did not debut with iPadOS 16 until later in the year. The program now includes additional tools including a watercolor brush, calligraphy pen, highlighter, variable-width pen, and ruler in addition to the Follow Along function, which allows you to view what your coworkers are working on. Additionally, form Recognition lets you to sketch a form by hand, such a square, and see it instantly take on the same shape you made with a tap.

Stage Manager
Another feature that debuted with iPadOS 16 was Stage Manager; you can learn more about it in our dedicated Stage Manager piece. However, for iPadOS 17, Stage Manager receives a small upgrade. You may arrange your workspace precisely as you want it since Stage Manager is now more adaptable when it comes to moving and resizing windows thanks to the software update.

Spotlight
With iPadOS 17, a new function called Top Hit is added to Spotlight search. This implies that Top Hit will present a smart secondary search result, such as your Favorites album when looking for Photos, when you use Spotlight to look for an app.

Photos
With iPadOS 17 updates, the Photos app is now better at recognizing your favorite people and will even recognize your dog and cat.

Siri
With iPadOS 17, good ol' Siri also receives an upgrade, allowing you to ask follow-up inquiries without having to say Hey Siri once again. Speaking of Hey Siri, you may just say "Siri" instead of "Hey" now.

AirPlay
With iPadOS 17, AirPlay also receives a few improvements, one of which is the ability to gradually learn your preferences. Later this year, AirPlay will also be accessible in compatible hotel rooms, enabling you to send photographs, movies, and music to the TV in your room by scanning a QR code and connecting to it.

Find My
With iPadOS 17, Find My has received an upgrade that now includes the ability to Share an AirTag with up to five people. When they are close to the shared AirTag, everyone in the group will be able to play the sound to find it.

AirDrop
With iPadOS 17 and iOS 17, there are a few new capabilities for AirDrop, including the capacity to carry on a file transfer through AirDrop even after you leave the area. When it is published, a transfer you start using AirDrop will continue over the internet while you walk away since it is not yet accessible because it will be a bit later.

Reminders
With iPadOS 17, the Reminders app also receives a few changes, including grocery lists that automatically group products into categories to make grocery shopping simpler. Additionally, a new Column View makes it simple to visualize your chores by organizing areas of your screen into columns.

Music
With iPadOS 17, the Music app also received an upgrade that allowed users to invite friends to playlists and work together to add, rearrange, and delete music. Emojis are another way to express your feelings about the songs that are being played right now.

AirPods
iPadOS 17 makes various enhancements to AirPods as well, including the addition of tap-to-mute functionality for AirPods Pro (2nd Generation), even though an iPad is not always directly involved. The AirPods Pro (2nd Generation) also have a Conversation Awareness mode and a function called Adaptive Audio that combines Transparency and Active Noise Cancellation. The improved Automatic transitioning feature makes transitioning between Apple devices easier and more smooth.

WHICH IPADS ARE COMPATIBLE WITH IPADOS 17?
Apple only discontinued support for the iPad Air (2nd gen) from 2014 and the iPad mini (4th gen) from 2015 for iPadOS 16. The iPad (fifth generation), iPad Pro 9.7-inch (first generation), and iPad Pro 12.9-inch (first generation) are the three devices that will no longer be supported with iPadOS 17. However, there are still 20 iPads that can run the software, six of which are included in our list of the best iPads.

With iPadOS 17, the following iPad models are compatible:
- iPad Pro (2nd generation and later)
- iPad (6th generation and later)
- iPad Air (3rd generation and later)
- iPad mini (5th generation and later)

HOW TO INSTALL IPADOS 17

Prioritizing your data's protection is essential before implementing any major updates. All crucial data, including valuable images, crucial business documents, and other sorts of data, are secured by a backup. There are several backup options available to you:
- iCloud: Utilize Apple's cloud storage to securely keep your info.
- Mac: On your Mac, choose a local backup.
- PC: Use your Windows computer as a backup.

Once your backup is secure, you may now install the newest version of iPadOS 17. As follows:
- You should have WiFi enabled and a power supply attached into your iPad.
- Navigate to Settings > General to update your software.
- Choose Install Now or Download and Install under the iPadOS 17 upgrade.
- Try again in a few hours if the iPadOS 17 update isn't available straight away.
- After entering your passcode and reading the terms, click "Continue."
- When your iPhone begins downloading and the installation process, there can be restarts.
- Configure your preferences by following the on-screen directions after the update is complete.

Once more, check back a few hours later if the iPadOS 17 update hasn't yet appeared. Certain apps can be briefly deleted if a notice during the upgrading asks for more space. Do not fear; these programs will automatically reinstall when the upgrade is complete.

APPLE WATCH SERIES 9

The Apple Watch Series 9 is a little bit simpler to operate thanks to Double Tap and a quicker Siri.
What's inside matters when it comes to the new Apple Watch Series 9, which has a starting price of $399 (£399, AU$649) and is now offered alongside the Apple Watch Ultra 2. That is the main lesson I've learned from using the Series 9 for a few days. It includes an updated processor that enables speedier Siri performance and new Double Tap gesture capabilities.

These upgrades set the Series 9 apart from the Series 8 from the previous year and improve the use of the Apple Watch. However, they are not impressive enough to persuade recent customers to upgrade.

NEW DOUBLE TAP GESTURE

I was excited to test Double Tap because Apple rarely ever introduces new motions to the Apple Watch. You activate this function by twice touching your thumb and index finger together, as the name would imply. You may take use of this to, among other things, dismiss a notice, stop your timer, or access widgets from the watch face. It is configured to carry out whatever the primary notification action is, whether that be ignoring your default reminder or text message answering.

A comparable gesture was already enabled by the Apple Watch's AssistiveTouch accessibility mode. However, Double Tap is integrated into every aspect of the Series 9's user interface, and thanks to its processor, the watch can handle this function continuously without affecting battery life. In contrast, the pinching function that is a component of the watch's accessibility choices may be adjusted to suit a user's needs.

Even though I'm using an early version of Double Tap, there is a slight learning curve. I use Double Tap the most to turn off timers, turn off alerts, and send hands-free text messages. Since I prefer to check the time and my workout progress before going to bed, this was very helpful when I was brushing my teeth. I clenched my fingers together to delete a notification that was obstructing my watch face so I wouldn't have to put down my toothbrush.

It's a straightforward use case, but it illustrates Double Tap's potential. When my hands are busy, such as when I'm cleaning, cooking, or even holding onto the subway pole on my way to work, being able to respond to a text message without touching my watch may also be helpful.

SIRI GETS FASTER

A quicker Siri experience is a further advantage of the new S9 processor in the Series 9. For two reasons, Siri can now respond to requests a little bit quicker. First, actions like setting alarms or timers that Siri can perform without consulting the internet now take place on the watch. Additionally, dictation is touted to be up to 25% more accurate, so Siri ought to understand you right away.

After switching from the Series 8, I noticed a change. I frequently use Siri to set timers and alarms, especially when I'm warming up for a workout. When using my Series 8 or the Series 6, which I purchased around three years ago, I frequently repeat myself. On Series 9, this hasn't happened as frequently as it once did. I also timed how long Siri takes on the Series 9 vs the Series 8 to reply to certain queries. I limited the questions I asked Siri for this test to those she could respond to without searching the internet for an answer. On the Series 9, Siri was quicker in virtually every situation

DESIGN

We also don't have any major design-related surprises. The design of the Apple Watch Series 9 is similar to that of earlier models, and it features a recognisable rectangular shape with two case sizes: 41mm and 45mm.

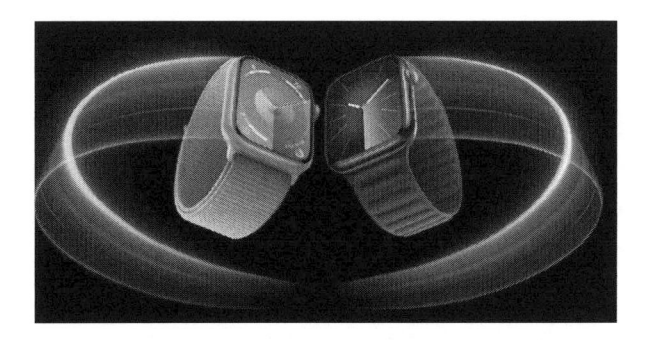

Aluminum and stainless steel are your options for the case material, which is rather normal. One distinction this year is that, to match the colors of the iPhone 15 this year, the Apple Watch Series 9 is also offered in pink in addition to its usual color selections. In addition, you receive Product (RED), Midnight, Silver, and Starlight.

NEW WATCH BANDS

Apple has recently aimed to be more environmentally friendly, and the corporation is now stepping it up. With the Series 9, Apple is doing away with the leather bands and replacing them with new eco-friendly watch bands. For starters, the Series 9 is Apple's first entirely carbon-neutral device, along with a redesigned Sport Loop. Additionally, new environmentally friendly items are part of the Nike and Hermès partnerships.

Apple has launched a new FineWoven material that will replace leather bands and is composed of 68% post-consumer recycled material. The leather bands will no longer be offered; instead, it comes with Magnetic Link and Modern Buckle bands.

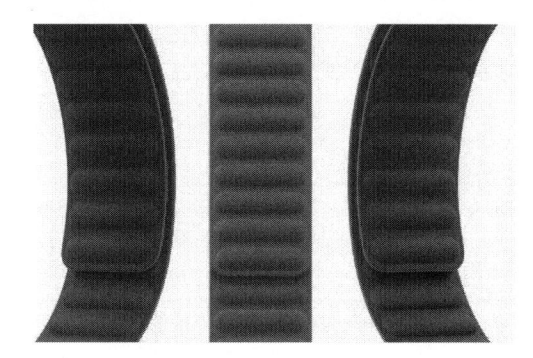

Battery
Apple needs to give battery life for Apple Watches some serious consideration. Although the Apple Watch Ultra and the new Ultra 2 have longer battery lives, not everyone wants to wear a watch that large all day (and night). The battery life of the Apple Watch has so far stayed largely constant. The Series 9 is experiencing the same thing this year.

The Series 9 has a battery life of up to 18 hours and a new Low Power Mode that can extend that up to 36 hours. With an Apple USB-C Magnetic Fast Charging Cable and a fast charging brick, the Series 8 can charge from zero to eighty percent in around 45 minutes, according to Apple's official documentation. The Series 9 is the same, and in our opinion, it's pretty good as well.

WATCHOS 10
Apple has released the first official image of the watchOS 10 software, which will be accessible on both your current Apple Watch and the next versions. This year's Worldwide Developer Conference (WWDC 2023) keynote speech featured a live demonstration of the software on stage. Different abilities were highlighted. So what is unique now?

NEW DESIGN FOR WIDGETS AND APPLICATIONS.
For Apple's watchOS 10, most of the regularly used basic apps, including the Weather app, Stocks app, Messages app, World Clock app, Apple Maps app, and default Phone app, have been completely redesigned. The Activity app will be updated with new sharing features, additional Apple Fitness+ connectivity, and a more eye-catching trophy case.

Soon, the Apple Watch will include a feature akin to Smart Stack that will allow you to organize significant widgets on the watch face. Widgets on iPhones are arranged using Smart Stack. By rotating the Digital Crown, the various widgets are displayed. The sequence in which they are presented is dynamic; for instance, the weather widget will be displayed first in the morning and the calendar will move to the top when a meeting is planned.

SNOOPY IS ONE OF THE NEW WATCH FACES.

There are several new watch faces in watchOS 10. The Portrait watch faces' depth perspective will also be used by the watch face for the Smart Stack widget. There is also a watch face called Palette that has an inventive and colorful way of showing the time. The best new watch face could be the two new characters, Snoopy and Woodstock. The Peanuts crew now joined the Toy Story family and Mickey Mouse on the Apple Watch, and together they will all interact with the watch face's hands, react to the weather, and even motivate you to start exercising.

HOW TO GET THE SNOOPY WATCH FACE USING YOUR IPHONE

You may access any watch face through the Face Gallery in the Apple Watch app and the Watch app on your iPhone if you're not familiar with the world of Apple Watch faces. We believe that using the Face Gallery is the most straightforward way to see every watch face that is available.

Although it is possible to install watch faces directly to your watch (we'll show you how to do that later), adding watch faces via the Watch app is more easier due to the larger screen size. You may customize an appealing watch face from the face gallery, such as Snoopy, Palette, or another one, choose complications (if available), and then apply the face to your watch.

Fire up the Watch app on your iPhone.

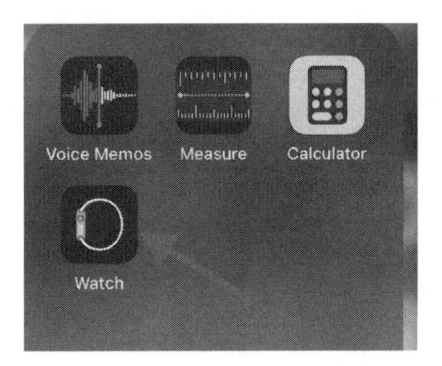

To display the watch faces you currently own, choose My Watch from the bottom tabs.
After that, click Edit on the right side of My Faces.

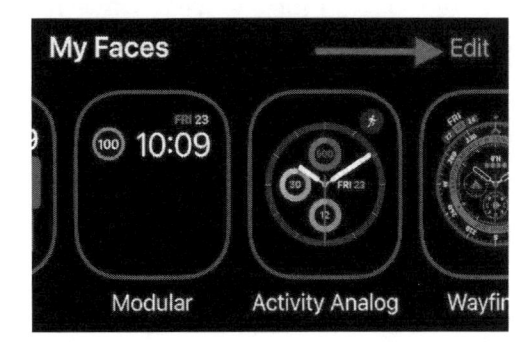

This lists every Apple Watch face that is installed on your watch right now. You can browse watch faces and get rid of any that you don't need. To remove a watch face from your smartphone, tap the minus symbol.

Select Face Gallery from the middle tab at the bottom of the screen.

Snoopy and the Palette Watch Face may be found here under New Watch Faces. Look for Snoopy and Palette if they aren't mentioned here by scrolling below.

Tap Snoopy and then select Add next to it on your Apple Watch to install the new Snoopy Face. You may decide on the background color and dial design for the watch face now or later, before adding it. Right now, Snoopy doesn't provide any difficulties.

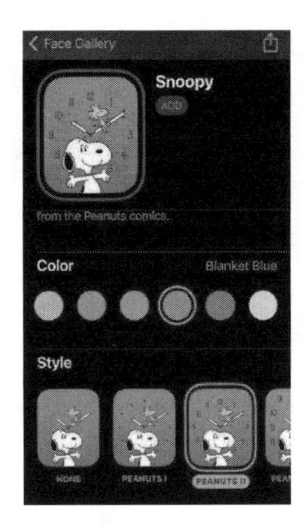

The Palette watch face and any other watch faces you select may be added to your watch using the same process.

HOW TO GET THE NEW SNOOPY WATCH FACE ON YOUR APPLE WATCH WITHOUT USING AN IPHONE
If your iPhone is not close by, such as if your phone is configured using Apple's family setup, you may still obtain the Snoopy Watch face.
Open your Apple Watch's current watch face.

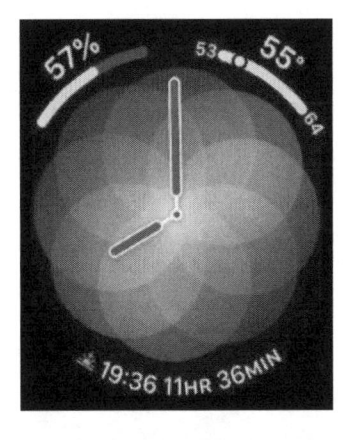

Long-press on the currently active watch face to open the watch face editor.

Swipe until you come across the option to add a new watch face. Press the plus sign.

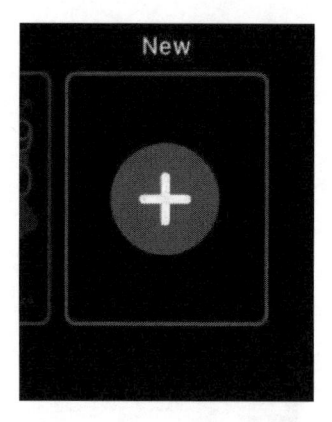

Search for the New Watch faces option or scroll down the list to discover the Snoopy watch face.

Tap the Add button to set Snoopy as your watch face!
Swipe left or right to change the color or dial style. The adjustment may then be made by turning the Digital Crown. To change the color of the backdrop, click Color and then use the Digital Crown to tweak the color option.

Press the Digital Crown to save your adjustments when you're done.
To make the watch face your current face, tap it.

CYCLING, GOLF, AND TENNIS MODES

WatchOS 10 includes changes to Apple's fitness monitoring system that are particular to cycling. It now calculates your Functional Threshold Power (FTP) score using information from your power, heart rate, and motion and shows how much time you spend in a series of personalized heart rate zones known as Power Zones in order to assist you in improving your cycling performance.

With watchOS 10, Bluetooth bike sensors are supported, and a new Live Activity widget will show all the data the Apple Watch is getting if you use an iPhone placed on a handlebar. It may be made full-screen or small enough to function as a running timer. Additionally, keep a look out for recent cadence and speed numbers. Developers will be able to utilize this data to improve the golf and tennis games since the Apple Watch will be able to track rapid changes in direction and speed.

HOW TO CONNECT BIKE SENSORS – CADENCE, SPEED, POWER

With watchOS 10, Apple no longer requires your sports software to manually set up the Bluetooth connections because it now natively supports them. You'll find that the Apple Workout app immediately establishes a connection with these sensors once your sensor and Watch are connected, enabling you to get started right away. Before you ride, don't forget to verify the accuracy of your power meter.

Control Centre

Utilize the Control Center on the Watch to locate the amusing triangle and concentric circle icon. From there, it is logically straightforward to choose the nearest sensors you want to connect to from a list.

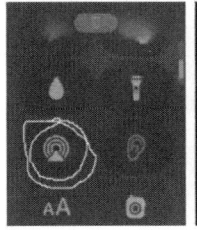

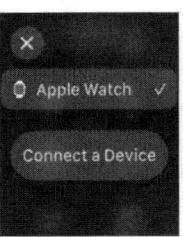

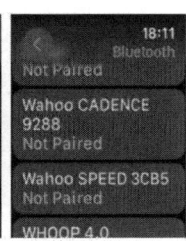

You can connect to many power meters, cadence sensors, speed sensors, and heart rate sensors, albeit the Watch will only use one of each type. Additionally, it's crucial to bear in mind that a single sensor could be capable of providing several cycle data kinds. For instance, a power meter could on occasion also provide cadence information. There are variations to different power meters, whether they transmit left and right energy separately, together, or visually appear to be two separate power meters. What you see will depend on the power meter model you have, but generally, EVERYONE SHOULD WORK WITH APPLE.

Configuration & Calibration

If you've got pedals for a power meter and a speed sensor attached, you might need to give the watch the tire measurements and vice versa. It is always advisable to double-check these values, even if, as was the case in my instance, the crank length had previously been properly changed in the Assioma (power meter) app.

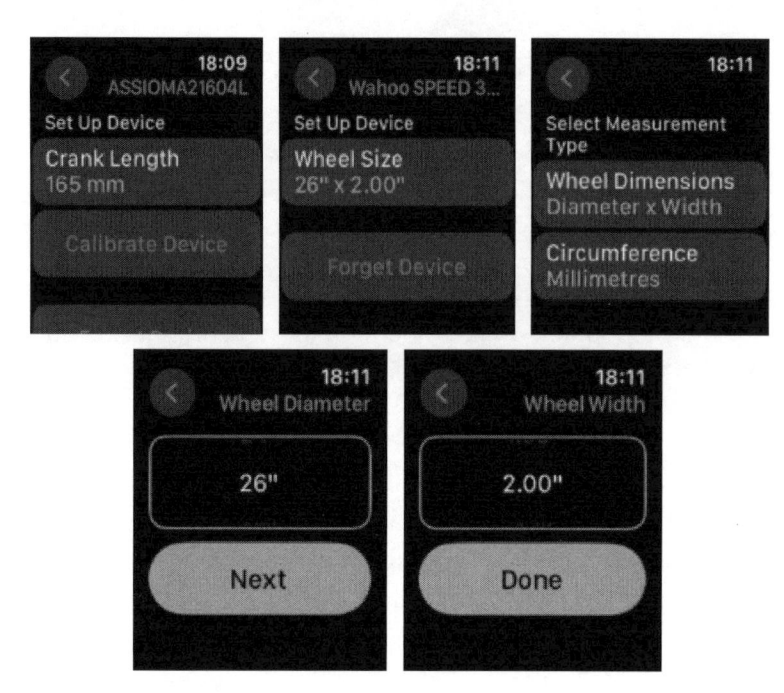

HOW TO USE YOUR IPHONE TO VIEW YOUR CYCLING STATISTICS

Another new feature of watchOS 10 is the capability to view your riding activity on your iPhone. This is helpful if you have an iPhone bike mount. Once your Apple Watch and iPhone are connected, you won't need to purchase those expensive cycle computers. As soon as you start cycling and launch the workout app on your Apple Watch, the cycling action will therefore display immediately on your iPhone. Apple allegedly made that assertion. To access this function, I needed to use the iPhone's Fitness app.

ENHANCEMENTS TO APPLE MAPS.

The Apple Maps app will get a brand-new topographic view with elevation, waypoints, and a search function. You may look for information on hiking routes, including specifics about their duration, height, and difficulty, before you head out. The topographic map will be made available in the U.S. initially, with other nations to follow. If you use Maps on your iPhone, watchOS 10 will provide access to the Apple Watch's offline features, including navigation, arrival time, locations, and more.

The compass app has been improved to provide hikers more destinations. The first specifies where your last cellular signal was so you may go back there if required, and the second defines where you can call an SOS from any carrier, not just your own. The compass view will also be available in 3D.

How to Use the Hiking Features in watchOS 10

Now that you are aware of what the hiking features in watchOS 10 are, let's look at how you may utilize them.

Waypoints and Elevation Views

To use cellular connectivity waypoints on your Apple Watch, you must first open the Compass app. You will notice these symbols when you arrive:
Your most recent cellular connection is indicated by the color green.
Red SOS logo: The address where you last called 911.

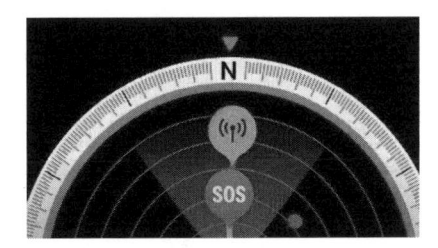

Your elevation will be shown at the bottom of the screen.

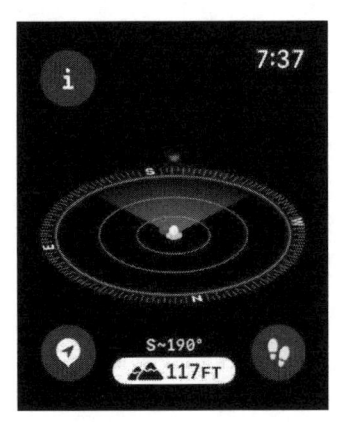

Looking for Nearby Trails

You may identify local trails and tourist attractions by using the Maps app on your Apple Watch. While there, stop by:

By pressing the search icon, you may find the Find Nearby section.
By clicking, choose Trails or Trailheads. Then, when you see a trek you want to go on, click the walking person icon.

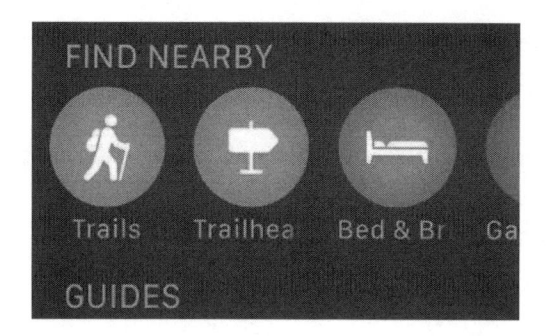

HOW TO USE TOPOGRAPHICAL MAPS
If you're in the US, simply open the Maps program to use the topographic map. In some aspects, it will resemble what you see below.
You should be aware that Topo Club is actually Apple Maps Club before anything else. Topographic maps are available in the on-watch Maps app but not in the Workouts app. The one that resembles the arrow up stuff you see in the centre of the screen is that one (the down-arrow one is for diving, and the up-compass arrow is for the compass):

This is significant since there is a clear distinction between the areas used for general navigation and those frequently used for workouts (the exercises app). The majority of people going on a hiking expedition would use the Workouts app to keep track of their workout data, so this is yet another app you'd need to switch between. Despite the fact that Apple makes it easy, it's not as easy as a fast swipe of the data page. All the action in this post takes place in the Apple Maps app, not the Workout app.

In any case, you'll be able to view your current location when it opens. If you were sitting at your desk at home in a level area, it's doubtful that you would see any topographic lines or features. You can only see the following types of maps:

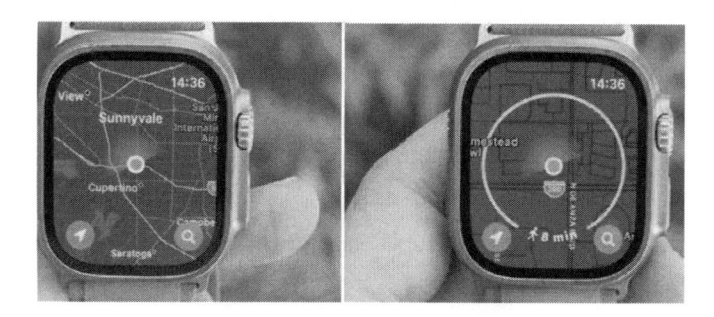

Instead, you ought to go to a place where there could be mountain lions. Yes, I am aware that most typical Californian towns have this, but we also need the "mountain" component. Scroll to certain hills to greatly zoom in. You have to suddenly expand the image to see it:

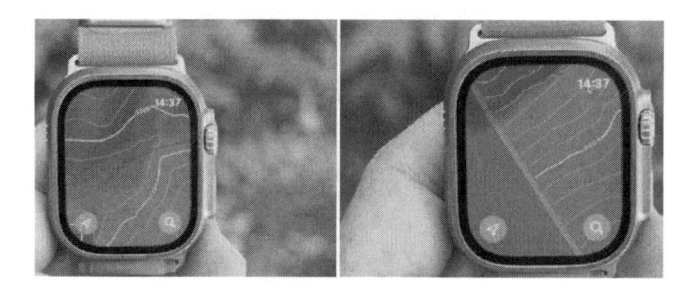

I could have been more explicit, but we should go to a place where there may be mountain lions. You must visit a California parkland that has been recognized as such in order to access the most recent beta (see above, right, where the topo lines end where the green does). Proclaimed parks that stretches from California into Nevada is also useful. But if it spreads to Oregon, that fails. Someone in Oregon insulted someone in Cupertino. I didn't make the beta Topo Club rules; I only describe them.

The current public beta requires you to find a suitable park in California if you want to examine topographic map data as of September 12th, 2023 at 10AM Cupertino time, to put it another way. Or, pretend to be a mountain lion that crossed the border from California to Nevada while remaining within the park's boundaries. Otherwise, no Topo Club for you. Here, you can see where the topo lines cease right before the Oregon-California border:

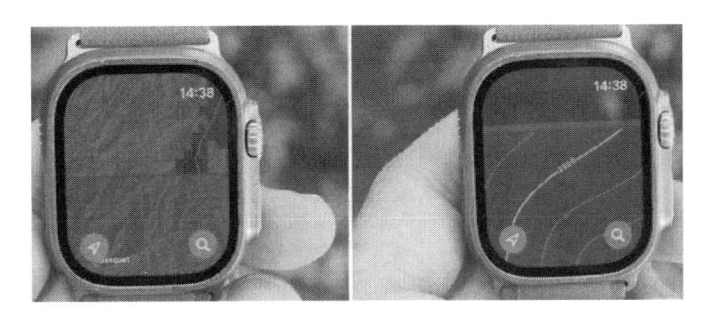

The topo lines for parks that stretch into Nevada continue: Just make sure it's a park that started somewhere in California.

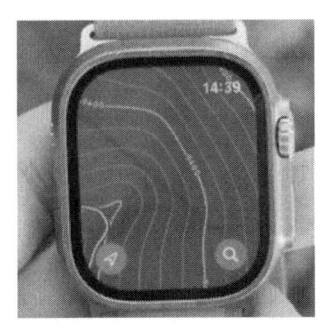

Apple has now openly said that it will only be produced for the US and not for other nations when it goes into production. But it's not clear if it will still be restricted to specific parklands. There are still significant tracts of very walkable ground without contour lines, even in California. The Pacific Shore Trail travels over a huge part of shore that is still barren of it.

Given the intricacies of how licensing and mapping data work, I'm sure this is a difficult topic. But even worldwide, all of Apple's competitors only provide "everywhere" topo maps. The US limitation is the only one of these gaps that none of their rivals in the endurance sports industry, including Garmin, Suunto, and COROS, have.

Next, let's be clear that the Apple Watch doesn't actually include offline topographic maps. Instead, the Apple Watch may access the offline topo maps saved on your phone if it is close by and turned on. or if you have access to cellular or WiFi. Select the locations you want to download offline topo maps for by opening Apple Maps on your phone, clicking your profile picture in the corner, and then scrolling down. This package also contains the topo maps. It's interesting to note that the Watch Maps app does seem to store certain non-topo pieces, but it's unclear exactly at what zoom level (and whether it is in park or not) it does so. You can download different parts if you'd like:

The major differences between Apple's approach to mapping and those of Garmin, Suunto, or COROS devices, which deliver real offline maps on your wrist, are once again brought to light by this. I don't see why Apple wouldn't cache those to the watch. Since the watch has so much capacity, as seen above, the file sizes are really small. The specification for offline versus non-offline mapping on watches differs significantly, too.

Contrarily, whereas Garmin has more precise levels of POIs and trail/street names on its maps, neither Suunto nor COROS do. Therefore, despite the various limitations, Apple really provides more information than Suunto/COROS in this situation. But at least the data is accessible.

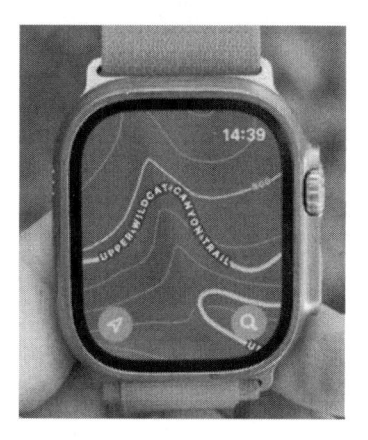

The next thing was presumably something you saw or remembered from the WatchOS 10 presentation a month ago—a trailhead with a suggested route to it. To achieve that, I'll show you two different things. I'll pick a trailhead that is currently nearby to begin with. Vehicle routing will be used as the default when I do that. By tapping: I may change that to a path for bicycles or pedestrians.

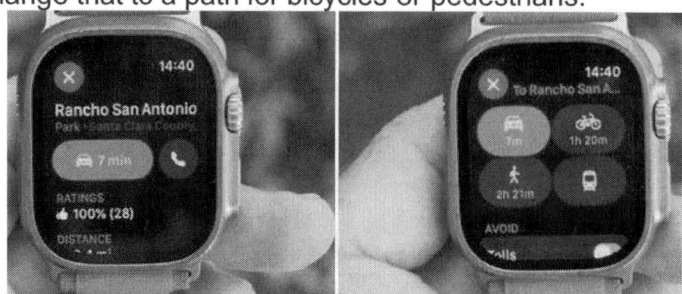

It now offers me a choice of route options along with elevation profiles, which is kind of cool:

It now offers me a choice of route options along with elevation profiles, which is kind of cool:

However, in order to create the turn-by-turn directions, you must first have internet access. Once the route is established, you no longer need internet (and it seems to preserve it for prior historical routes as well).
Let's set internet connectivity aside for a second and say that you don't have to choose a trailhead (or gas station). I'll place a pin there and then navigate to the summit of this park as an example. You'll see that it does as I would expect and follows the trails:

This works well in situations that are point-to-point (destination-based), but it is plainly useless while hiking or in other situations when a loop or other preset path is employed. Routes and courses cannot presently be added directly to Apple; instead, they must all be added via third-party applications.

You may see some of the several teams at work here. Despite the fact that all of Apple's recent marketing campaigns (particularly those focused on Ultra) are targeted towards endurance sports, the topographic maps come from the Apple Maps team. In this case, only an Apple Watch app (Maps) is necessary, and that team is independent of the Apple Watch team. And that program is effectively simply a scaled-down version of Apple Maps' primary mobile program. It should be a phone-first experience rather than one that is watch-first.

The Apple Watch Series 9 can now more easily locate your iPhone.

If you're anything like me, you've used the Apple Watch to locate a misplaced iPhone that got caught between the couch cushions. Apple added a second-generation ultra-wideband processor to the watch to improve its functionality as an iPhone locator. The Series 9 gives you a nudge in the right direction and an estimate of your distance from your phone in addition to allowing you to ping your iPhone.

The catch is that this feature is only accessible if you own one of the iPhone 15 or iPhone 15 Pro as only those models have the new ultra-wideband CPU. Therefore, unless you plan to buy a new iPhone along with your Apple Watch, you won't be able to use it.

Mental health and Mindfulness

With iOS 17, Apple is emphasizing mental health and providing tools to aid in self-evaluation. This is included in watchOS 10 as well. You may monitor your feelings and mood throughout the day with the Mindfulness app for the Apple Watch. By moving the Digital Crown, you may choose phrases and shapes that go with how you are feeling. The program has the same recognized appearance as the Mindfulness app.

It's exciting that Apple will provide clinically useful personal evaluations that let you submit data and assess your own risk of treatable illnesses like depression. It will also point you in the direction of groups that can help you, depending on your level of risk. This will also be a feature of the iPhone's Health app starting with iOS 17.

Vision Health

By using the Apple Watch in a unique way, myopia, or nearsightedness, will be averted in children. The Apple Watch's ambient light sensor will monitor how much time kids spend outside, which is important for preventing the onset of myopia. Even if your child doesn't have an iPhone, the information is still available through the Family Sharing app.

Furthermore, it will be simpler to gauge how distant a screen on a gadget is from you. A warning that suggests moving further away from an iPhone or iPad that detects that you are too near to it will appear, helping to further reduce the risk of eye strain and other problems down the road. Using iOS 17's NameDrop feature, a fast click of the exchange button on watchOS 10 will send your personal contact sheet to an iPhone or another Apple Watch, making it quick and easy to share contact information.

Users of the Apple Watch may use the FaceTime app to participate in FaceTime Audio chats and see video messages on the watch's screen. A new update to the Medications app will send a reminder if you haven't confirmed an activity, like taking a pill, after 30 minutes, while Apple Fitness+ will get Custom Plan.

AirPods Pro

When used with second-generation AirPods Pro that have been upgraded with the newest firmware, the additional functions are available on iPhones running iOS 17. Both the new USB-C MagSafe Charging Case and the Lightning MagSafe Charging Case for the second-generation AirPods Pro fall under this category.

How to Check Your AirPods Pro Firmware

when firmware for AirPods is often installed over-the-air when the AirPods are attached to an iOS device, Apple does not provide instructions on how to do so. The update should be forced by placing the AirPods in their case, plugging them into a power source, and then pairing them with an iOS device or Mac. Following these instructions while connected to your iPhone will allow you to check the firmware on your AirPods Pro:

- Launch the Settings app.
- Tap the AirPods Pro with [your name].
- To find the "About" section, scroll below.

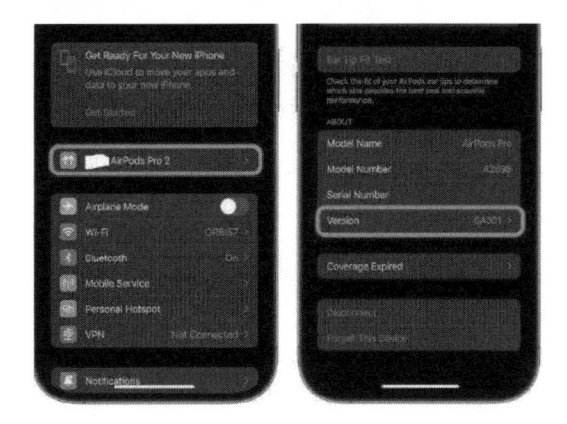

Search for the version 6A301.
You are prepared to use the new capabilities in iOS 17 if your AirPods Pro have the most recent software (as of September 2023) and the right version number.

ADAPTIVE AUDIO

The Adaptive Transparency feature of the second-generation AirPods Pro provides a novel technique to lessen strong background noise for more comfortable everyday listening when it was first released. By dynamically combining the current Transparency and Active Noise Cancellation modes, Adaptive Audio, or Adaptive Noise Control, raises that method to a new level and provides the optimum audio quality at any given time. Adaptive Audio adjusts the noise cancellation when you switch between various settings and interactions.

The sound of a leaf blower, for example, is automatically muted in this fashion, but other loud or irritating noises like a sudden automobile horn blast remain audible.

- Connect your AirPods Pro to your iPhone and follow one of these instructions to enable or disable Adaptive Audio.
- Launch Settings.
- Tap the AirPods Pro with [your name].

Under "Noise Control," tap Adaptive.

CONVERSATION AWARENESS

Conversation Awareness is able to recognize when someone begins speaking to you and will adjust the audio level and background noise accordingly. By decreasing background noise as you speak, Conversation Awareness also helps while you're on a call. This function, which is a part of Adaptive Audio, also amplifies the voices in front of you so you can hear what is being said. Connect your AirPods Pro 2 to your iPhone and then follow these instructions to enable or disable Conversation Awareness.

- Launch Settings.
- Tap the AirPods Pro with [your name].
- Toggle the switch next to Conversation Awareness on or off in the "Audio" section by scrolling down.

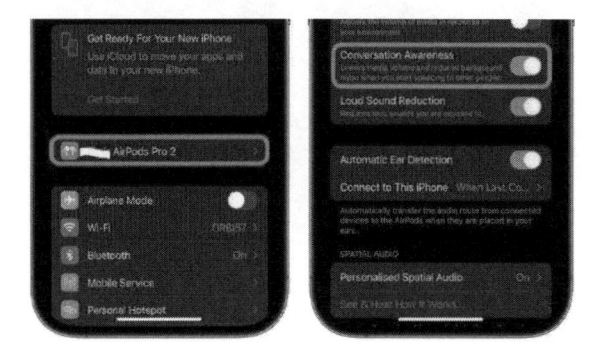

PERSONALIZED VOLUME

In a manner similar to Adaptive Audio, Personalized Volume employs machine learning to optimize your listening experience by recognizing listening preferences and contextual factors.

This function enables your iPhone to gradually learn about the volume you prefer and adjust it as necessary to fit your preferred sound level.

Connect your AirPods Pro 2 to your iPhone, then follow these instructions to set or disable Personalized Volume.

- Launch Settings.
- Tap the AirPods Pro with [your name].
- In the "Audio" section, scroll down and turn the switch next to Personalized Volume on or off.

MUTE CONTROLS

AirPods Pro haven't had an assignable on-board mute feature up until now. But that's no longer the case with iOS 17. While you're on a call, you may mute and unmute yourself by pressing the stem of your AirPods Pro headphones.

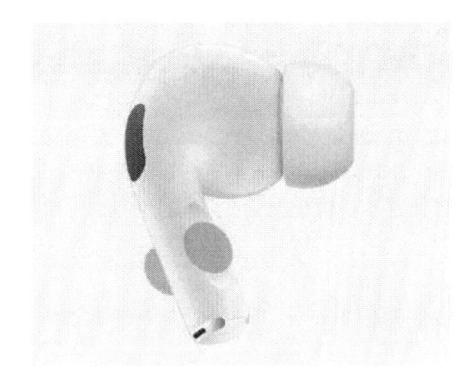

On your iPod Pro 2, you may program the mute and unmute call controls to operate with either a single push or a double press of the button. To select a preference, connect your AirPods Pro 2 to your iPhone and proceed as directed.

- Launch Settings.
- Tap the AirPods Pro with [your name].
- Tap Mute & Unmute after swiping down to "Call Controls" in the list.
- Choose between pressing once or twice.

Chapter 7: CarPlay

Apple CarPlay is the company's solution to the issue of utilizing mobile apps while driving, two activities that don't often mix well. Because your phone has a number of helpful features and applications that may help you while you're driving, and because CarPlay works with Google's Android Auto, you can use them without endangering other drivers.

Simply put, CarPlay beams the applications from your phone onto the infotainment screen in your car, replete with hands-free operation and a user-friendly interface. This means you may navigate, make calls or send texts, manage your music, and do so much more without endangering other drivers. What can you actually do with the driving-friendly software, and how does it operate? Here is all the information you want regarding Apple CarPlay.

Which iPhones are compatible with CarPlay?

Every iPhone launched since the late 2012 debut of the iPhone 5 supports CarPlay. All the way up to the most recent iPhone 15 series, this includes more affordable gadgets like the iPhone 5C and original iPhone SE. It goes without saying that you cannot utilize CarPlay if you own an Android phone or an iPad or iPod.

Which cars offer CarPlay integration?

When it was introduced in 2014, CarPlay was a very specialized piece of software, but it has now become widely used in the automotive sector. Given this, it will be difficult to find a car manufacturer that doesn't provide CarPlay in some capacity, and much harder to find a current vehicle that doesn't have it. Almost all of the major automakers support CarPlay, which is presently available in more than 600 vehicles. The list of Apple Car-compatible vehicles provides information on the automakers and models that enable CarPlay. However, it's always a good idea to confirm CarPlay functionality for any vehicle you're considering purchasing.

Tesla stands out as a clear exception to this trend because it doesn't allow Android Auto or CarPlay. Instead, the manufacturer of all-electric vehicles provides its own high-end connection package, which includes navigation, streaming, and remote control of some systems. While CarPlay is free and uses your existing data plan, this does cost $10 a month.

As more vehicles operate on the new Android Automotive OS, they are now turning to Google for their software requirements. Android Automotive is a built-in feature of the automobile, as opposed to Android Auto, which is an app similar to CarPlay. This eliminates the need for any custom software. But if you own an iPhone, what does this mean?

The good news is that even if your car uses the Android Automotive OS, CarPlay will still function. You may plug your iPhone in and use it as usual if the automaker supports it for that specific model, like Polestar does with the Polestar 2.

Can I get CarPlay in the car I already own?

There are several methods for retrofitting CarPlay into a car, but some of them are trickier than others. The easiest option is to get a separate display that works with CarPlay and doesn't need to be retrofitted into your car in any significant manner.

It's important to note that Apple does not offer a specific driving mode for iPhones or a single CarPlay app, in contrast to Android. There is a Driving Focus mode that disables phone distractions while you are driving, but there is no mode that enables you to utilize a CarPlay-like interface on your phone.

There are gadgets like the Intellidash Plus that allow you to connect in your phone and use CarPlay. Though you'll need to find a spot to put the screen so it's both helpful and doesn't obstruct your view of the road, functionally it's the same as if you bought a car with CarPlay built-in. Alternately, you could always replace the factory-installed display/navigation system in your car with an aftermarket device if you'd prefer something a bit more streamlined. All you have to do is be prepared to go through the hassle of replacing your old unit with a new one.

Additionally, it depends on your ability to actually improve your automobile, which isn't a given. Additionally, keep in mind that many aftermarket devices demand a double DIN slot, although many older vehicles might only have one. There are single-DIN CarPlay devices available, however the selection you have is entirely based on your vehicle.

Prices can vary here, but you should expect to pay at least a few hundred dollars. While more sophisticated models like the wireless Kenwood Excelon DNX997XR or the 10.1-inch Pioneer-WT8600NEX may cost upwards of $1,500, versions like the Pioneer DMH-1500NEX cost little under $500. Of course, installation expenses must also be taken into account. Because you should probably leave this type of work in the skilled hands of a professional. Realistically speaking, it could be worthwhile to get a separate monitor in order to avoid the hassle.

How do you connect your iPhone to CarPlay?

There are two methods to connect your iPhone to CarPlay, with the simplest being to use a Lightning cable to connect it to the USB connection in your car. After you connect, CarPlay will appear on the screen of your vehicle, and all of your compatible applications will be updated. Wireless CarPlay is supported by several automobiles. When CarPlay initially starts, if you have one of them, your phone will invite you to set up a wireless connection; this will happen automatically on subsequent trips.

How to set up wireless Apple CarPlay via USB

Use a Lightning cable to connect your phone to the USB-A port on the vehicle. Make sure the display is powered on and the ignition is turned on.

As soon as CarPlay is activated, your phone and automobile should instantly connect. If not, check the applications menu in your car for a specific Apple CarPlay or smartphone connection option.

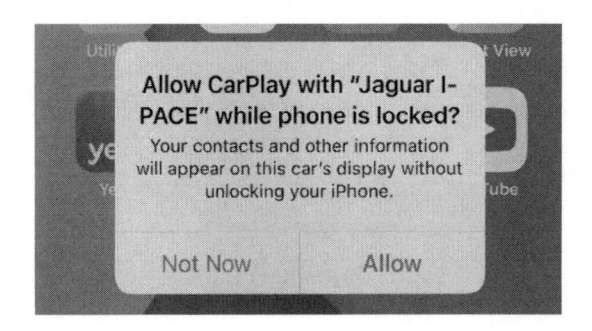

When your phone is locked, it will prompt you to approve CarPlay use. Click Allow.

The next screen asks if you want to Enable Wireless CarPlay if your car supports it. Tap it. Check to see if the CarPlay connection remains after unplugging your phone. If it does, make sure Bluetooth is turned on in both your car and iPhone. Every time you start the car after the wireless connection is established, CarPlay should launch instantly.

How to set up wireless Apple Carplay wirelessly
Do not worry if your vehicle does not support wired CarPlay or if you do not have a USB-A to Lightning cable on hand. Without a wire, you may install CarPlay by using the voice command capabilities of your vehicle.
While the wireless or Bluetooth is turned on, press and hold the voice command button on the steering wheel.
Go to Settings > General > CarPlay on your iPhone.

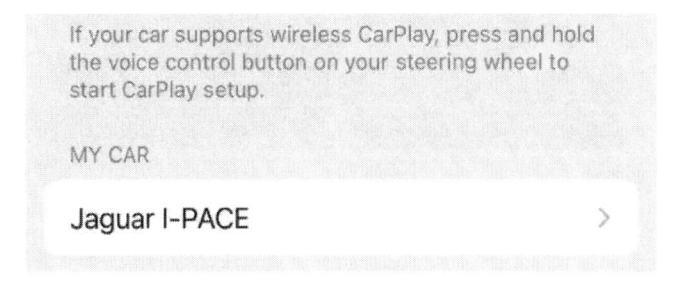

Locate and choose your vehicle.
Once it has initialized, CarPlay will keep doing so each time you start your engine.

What apps work with CarPlay?
CarPlay supports a wide number of applications, many of which are, predictably, Apple-owned. There are several other third-party CarPlay applications available in addition to the standard Maps, Phone, Messages, Music, and so forth. Apple does not provide a full list of CarPlay-compatible applications, but

there are still plenty of choices. However, since these applications must be user-friendly for driving, you won't discover anything that's very distracting or necessitates prolonged eye contact. Therefore, there will be no Netflix, Apple TV Plus, gaming, etc.

Instead, the apps may be divided into a few broad groups: communication, audio, and navigation. You may thus use a variety of applications, including well-known ones like Audible, Spotify, and TuneIn, to listen to music, podcasts, audiobooks, and internet radio. Waze and Google Maps are also compatible with CarPlay, so you don't have to use Apple Maps. In the event that they urgently need to locate an electric vehicle charger, EV owners will also have access to applications like PlugShare. Additionally, applications like WhatsApp let you use just your voice to place calls or send messages.

The simplest approach to determine whether CarPlay is compatible with a certain app is to plug in your phone and check. There isn't a clear method to filter the results when looking for "CarPlay" on the app store, but you will find several alternatives there that you may not have known about. However, you shouldn't encounter too many problems if you tend to stay with the well-known applications.

How is Siri integrated with CarPlay?

Siri is a crucial component of the CarPlay system since it allows you to command what is happening verbally. In this manner, you can keep your hands on the steering wheel and avoid accidentally pressing a touchscreen.
Siri functions exactly the same as when you use your phone regularly. Simply use the "hey Siri" wakeup command to alert the device and state your requirements. Siri can assist you whether you want to send a text message, adjust the music, or find the location of the closest gas station.
Siri, on the other hand, requires a live data connection because it is an internet-connected tool. Additionally, because Siri is connected to the cloud, there can be a little delay between your orders and their execution.

Chapter 8: Maintenance and Troubleshooting

Even Apple's iPhones, which many consider to be the pinnacle of smartphone design and are exquisitely made technological marvels, occasionally have issues.

Troubleshooting and Maintenance Practices

Restart Your iPhone
Turning the gadget off and back on is the most effective treatment for any electronic sickness, whether it affects iOS or Android, Windows or Mac, a TV or printer. In fact, there are very few circumstances in which a straightforward reboot shouldn't be your first option. The method functions because it restores the program to a stable condition after an unforeseen chain of circumstances led to a malfunction. Depending on the type of your iPhone, the procedure differs, but we've covered how to restart each iPhone.

Update iOS
If simple restart didn't resolve your problem, you must make sure your iPhone is up to date. Some iOS applications and features might not work with an older version of the operating system, in addition to the security risks this entails.

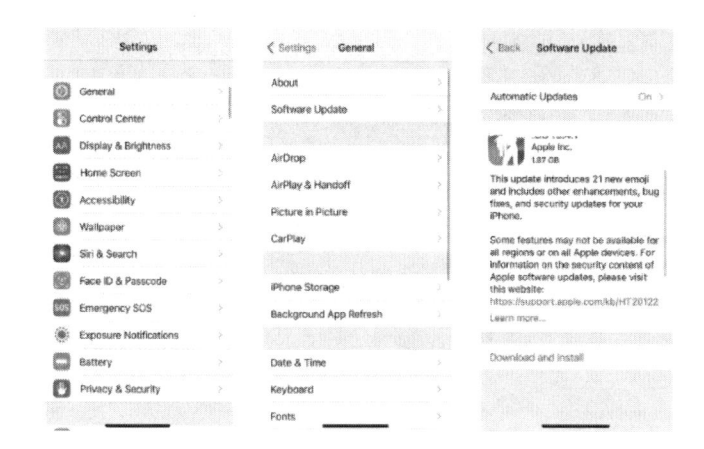

Go to Settings > General > Software upgrade to upgrade iOS.

Update Your Apps
It's important to make sure you're using the most recent version of an app if you're experiencing problems with it. This is because programmers frequently provide bug patches along with each new version, so the problem you're experiencing could already have been resolved. Through the App Store, you may manually update applications. Tap your profile picture at the top of the App Store app. After that, scroll down and select Update All or a particular app.

Force-Close an iPhone App
The instance of an app can occasionally stop responding, causing it to freeze.
Force-Close an App on iPhone X or Later
On an iPhone X, swipe up from the bottom of the screen while keeping your finger on the screen halfway up to force-quit an app. The app switcher will start on the phone. To close an app card, swipe up on it.
Force-Close an App on iPhone SE, iPhone 8, or Earlier
Double-press the home button on an iPhone 8 or before to open the app switcher and close an app forcibly. Locate the app you want to close by swiping left and right, then slide up.

Reset Your iPhone's Network Settings
Your network settings may be reset to resolve the majority of connectivity difficulties. Easy to accomplish.
To reset network settings, go to Settings > General > Transfer or Reset iPhone.

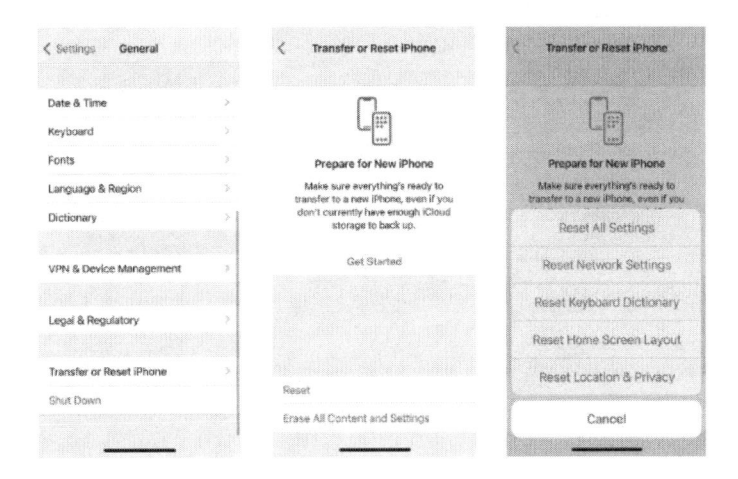

Although you won't lose any important data by doing this reset, you will lose any saved Wi-Fi passwords.

Reset All Settings on Your iPhone
You can reset all phone settings without losing your data if you believe that a wrong setting (rather than software or hardware) is the cause of your issues. Naturally, you'll have to return everything to its original configuration afterward.
To start, navigate to Settings > General > Transfer or Reset iPhone > Reset > Reset All Settings.

Factory Reset Your iPhone
You could factory reset your iPhone if you needed to take drastic measures. Your device will be restored to its initial state. Although this won't fix hardware issues, it ought to fix the majority of OS and software-related difficulties.

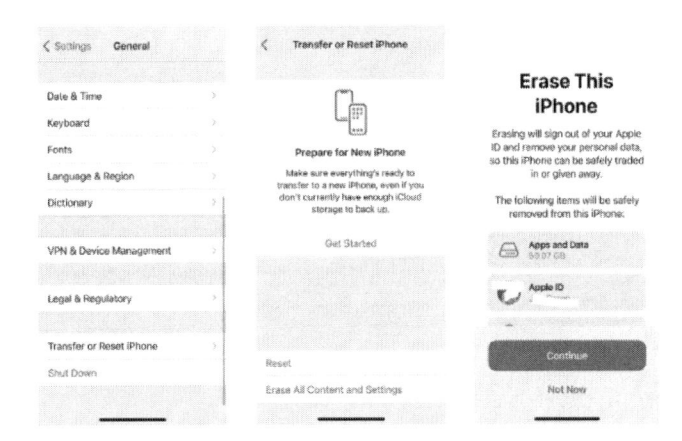

Open Settings > General > Transfer or Reset iPhone > Erase All Content and Settings to reset your iPhone.

Check Your iPhone's Battery Usage

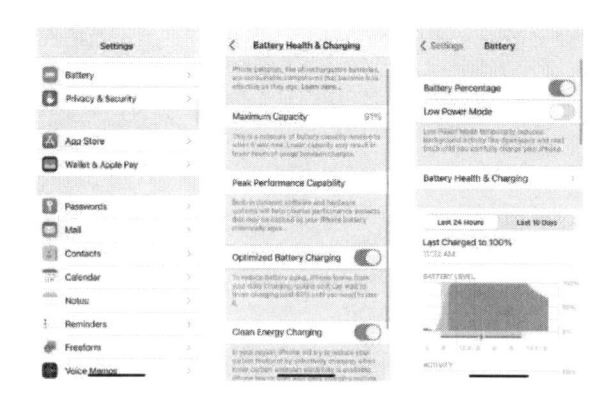

Even for heavy users, iPhones often offer good battery life. However, if the battery life of your cellphone is exceptionally short, you can try to pinpoint the problematic app. Go to Settings > Battery to find out which apps are the most energy-hungry. To view the battery use of various apps over a specified time period, check out the charts at the bottom.

Review Your iPhone's Battery Health
Before really degrading, batteries can only withstand a specific number of charge cycles. Fortunately, Apple makes it simple for you to monitor the battery life of your iPhone.
To check, navigate to Settings > Battery > Battery Health and Charging. And if it's less than 80%, a new battery has to be purchased.

Fix Bluetooth Issues
For a technology that is so extensively utilized, Bluetooth can occasionally behave surprising fussy. There are a few remedies you may attempt if you're having trouble setting up a Bluetooth connection between your iPhone and another device.
First, get rid of any outdated technology. It may aid in preventing disputes. Go to Settings > Bluetooth > Info > Forget This Device to unpair a device.
Next, restart Bluetooth (does this sound familiar?). To reach the Control Center and toggle Bluetooth, slide up from the bottom of the screen on an iPhone 8 or previous (swipe down from the upper-right on an iPhone X or after).

Fix HomeKit Issues
Some smart home appliances support HomeKit, allowing you to use Siri on your iPhone to operate them. Check to see if you're signed into the same iCloud account on both your iPhone and the HomeKit devices itself if they're not functioning as you would expect. Resetting your HomeKit connections may be done by navigating to Settings > Privacy & Security > HomeKit > Reset HomeKit Configuration if everything else fails.

Revoke Background Permissions
You can't utilize features like the camera flash on an overheated iPhone. In severe circumstances, using your phone can be impossible until it cools off.
It's obvious who the culprit is if you unintentionally left your phone in the sun. Overheating can also be caused by car vent clamps. However, if it frequently overheats while being used normally, a resource-intensive background software may be at blame. Go to Settings > General > Background program Refresh and move the toggles as needed for each program to stop operating in the background.

COMMON ISSUES AND SOLUTIONS

iPhones unquestionably excel when it comes to offering a fluid and flawless performance. That doesn't mean, though, that Apple's much-discussed smartphone hasn't seen its fair share of problems. Fortunately, there are a few useful tips and tactics that might resolve some of the frequent issues that occasionally plague the iPhone.

IPHONE BLACK SCREEN OF DEATH

The iPhone black screen of death occurs when even the Apple logo does not display in specific circumstances. You should attempt restarting your iPhone as a first step in solving this issue, which might be brought on by a botched update, jailbreak, or hardware issue. You might have to choose a hard reset (factory reset) for your iPhone if this is ineffective in any manner. You might need to do a DFU (device firmware update) boot for your iPhone if a hard reset does not help.

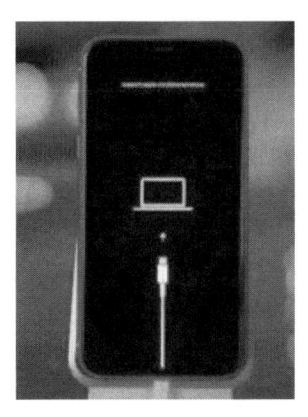

You shouldn't try this if you don't have an iCloud or iTunes backup since you risk losing your settings and data. Therefore, be sure to have a backup plan or contact a specialist that can assist you in solving this issue.

OVERHEATING ISSUES

You occasionally may receive a notice stating something to the effect of "iPhone needs to cool down before you can use it." This often indicates that your iPhone is getting too hot and that this might create difficulties. You need to be aware of the situation since there have been situations in the past where an iPhone just burst or caught fire due to the internal heating.

To fix this issue, move your smartphone to a cooler location, try turning off a few apps and the Bluetooth, and then begin the recovery process. Next, take the case or cover off your iPhone and put it away for a while.

The 'Reset All Settings' option on your phone can also be used to swiftly and permanently resolve this problem. You can also solve this issue by updating to a new version of iOS. You must get in touch with the specialists for assistance if the issue remains after attempting all of these solutions.

IPHONE CAMERA ROLL CRASH

Although they are uncommon, camera roll crashes can happen when there is not enough storage or other similar problems. A crash of your iPhone's camera roll might result in the loss of hundreds of images that were saved on the device. Additionally, this could make it impossible to do anything with the currently available collection of images and movies.

How can we solve this? Restoring the iPhone to factory settings is the first step. However, as you are aware, returning to factory settings would result in the total loss of all data, including contacts, chat messages, notes, photographs, videos, and more. So, only do that after taking a backup. Sync your iPhone using iTunes or iCloud. In the event that you are unable to connect to iCloud or iTunes, you can utilize third-party iPhone data recovery software. An professional who can complete this task for you can assist you.

ITUNES ERROR 3194

Thousands of iPhone customers encounter the iTunes 3194 Error, despite the fact that we don't see it frequently. You may see the iTunes 3194 issue when attempting to upgrade or restore your iPhone. It can be brought on by using the incorrect firmware version, an iOS version that is incompatible with your device, or by attempting to jailbreak your way inside.

The iPhone's host files provide the answer to this problem, thus some adjustments must be performed there in order to fix the problem. The other solution is to perform a "factory reset" on your smartphone, as we mentioned for many other issues.

WIFI IS NOT GETTING CONNECTED

iPhone or Wifi Is Not Connecting One of the main iPhone issues and fixes that many people run across is Wi-Fi being sluggish. Really, the answer is really straightforward. You only need to turn it off before restarting the phone. Press and hold the lock and home buttons at the same time until the Apple logo appears on the screen. You ought to be able to establish a WiFi connection when the phone has rebooted. If the problems still exist, go to Settings, choose WiFi, and then go to the bottom of the screen to adjust the HTTP proxy to automatic settings.

CELLULAR CONNECTION NOT WORKING ON IPHONE

Your iPhone's cellular connection could not be functioning for a number of reasons. A network issue on your iPhone, for instance, might be the cause of the issue. Therefore, if you have this problem, make sure that your location is not experiencing an outage and that your cellular connection is stable.

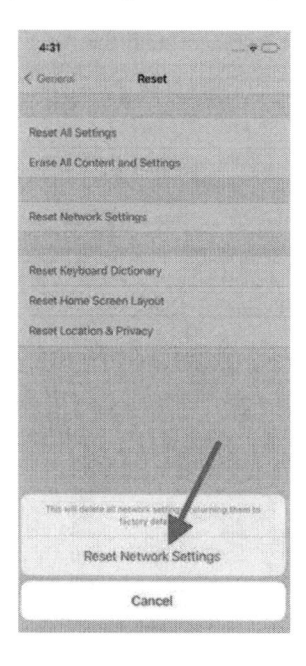

If the issue persists, you can reset the network configuration to fix the slow network. To accomplish this, open your device's Settings app and select General. At this point, touch Reset and choose Reset Network Settings. Once the network has been successfully reset, determine whether the issue has been resolved.

IPHONE IS STUCK AT APPLE LOGO
The iPhone gets stuck at Apple logo issue is one of the most prevalent issues that a lot of iPhone customers encounter. Fortunately, a force restart usually solves this issue. Therefore, hard reset your smartphone if it ever encounters this issue.

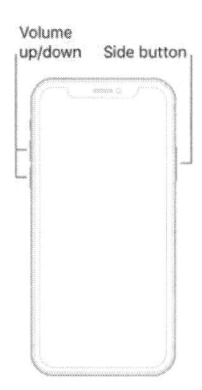

iPhone 8 and later: Press the volume up button to do a hard reset. Press the volume down button after that. Hold the side button down now until the Apple logo appears on the screen.
Press and hold the side button and the volume down button simultaneously for a few seconds until the Apple logo appears to perform a hard reset on an iPhone 7 or iPhone 7 Plus.
Hold down the power and home buttons at the same time for a few seconds until the Apple logo displays to perform a hard reset on an iPhone 6s or earlier.

IPHONE APP FREEZING/CRASHING RANDOMLY
In all honesty, the most of us have experienced app stalling and crashing at some point or another. The good news is that it's simple to resolve. Most often, older programs tend to stop or crash. So, check to see if the app has the most recent update (go to App Store > Profile). Once that's done, go to the app you wish to update. After that, click Update.

DAMAGE DUE TO WATER

Water is a nightmare for any electronic devices, and this is also true for iPhones. Don't panic if your phone falls into the water; there are various ways you may attempt before giving up. After removing the phone from the water, the first thing to do is to use a tissue paper to wipe up all of the excess water.
Never attempt to turn on the phone right away since doing so causes irreparable damage. The following step is to place your phone within a cup of rice. Within 24 hours, the rice will absorb the leftover liquid. The phone may also be physically disassembled and dried, although this requires some skill. You can get in touch with the closest service provider if the phone is still not functioning.

Apple Watch Seniors Guide

Conclusion

This seemed like an appropriate moment to see the iPhone 15/15 Plus and examine what this "first tier" model delivers with its equivalent in the Android world, with Google's next-generation flagship releasing just around the horizon. In essence, the iPhone 15 and iPhone 15 Plus are the iPhone 15 Pro and iPhone 15 Pro Max with the exception of new features like an Action Button and a periscope camera. With the exception of the telescopic camera, they too have colorful colors and Pro-level guts from last year.

I've been using the Google Pixel 7 together with the iPhone 15, however it will stop working once Google releases the Pixel 8. Similar drawbacks to Google's non-Pro model affect the iPhone 15, such as the latter's restricted magnification caused by the absence of a third lens. But it also shines in areas where the Pixel 8 may hope to follow. I don't worry about leaving the house with a USB-C cable because of the battery life, and the front-facing camera is one of the best for TikTok selfie rants. And isn't it great that the iPhone now supports USB-C? My Android and Apple review devices may share cords.

This is the right time to think about updating your iPhone if you've been holding out for at least three years. Even with its slightly weak USB-C connector, the iPhone 15 is a wonderful bundle starting at $800. Although the Pro model variation has all the bells and whistles, it costs $200 extra for features that aren't essential—an Action Button is only pleasant to have rather than being essential. The only additional item you could need is a telephoto lens, but as I already mentioned, if you want to wow people on Instagram, don't start at this pricing range.

For its storage options, the iPhone 15/15 Plus is also a worthwhile upgrade from wherever you are right now. If you're upgrading from an entry-level iPhone from a few generations back, you'll instantly have twice the storage capacity. For capturing high-resolution films and photographs, that 64GB allowance is just insufficient. The iPhone 15 has storage options starting at 128GB and going all the way up to 512GB. Again, the lack of telephoto capabilities on the lower-tier iPhone is the one significant disadvantage.